watch
over
me

tara sivec

Table of Contents

For Mom.

✝

God saw you getting tired
and a cure was not to be
so he put his arms around you
and whispered,
"Come to Me"
With tearful eyes we watched you
and saw you pass away
and although we love you dearly
we could not make you stay.
A Golden heart stopped beating
hard working hands at rest.
God broke our hearts to prove to us
He only takes the best. - Rhonda Braswell

Prologue

Death changes everyone.

It changes the way you think, the way you feel, and the way you live your life. Sometimes it makes you thankful for what you have, but more often than not, it makes you regret the things you've lost.

I'm eighteen years old and I've spent the better part of five months in a black hole that I can't seem to claw my way out of. Every breath I take, every moment in time I experience, is another reminder that the one person who should be here with me, guiding me and supporting me, is gone.

It's Mother's Day, five months since I lost her, since I lost myself to the memories and no longer recognize the girl staring back at me in the mirror. I woke up this morning knowing what I need to do but hating it so much I want to scream and rage at the unfairness of it all. The fact that I'm still not one hundred percent sure about my decision should be a sign that I'm not ready to do this. I have no other choice, though. There is no other place I need to go, no other person I want to be with.

The sky is overcast and there is a chill in the air. It's the perfect type of weather for my mood and my plans. I roll out of bed and throw on a ratty pair of shorts and one of her shirts that I kept. I slide my feet into flip-flops and drive to the Panera Bread by my house. I order her favorite: a cinnamon crunch bagel, toasted with butter, and a large hazelnut coffee with cream, no sugar, and tell the cashier it's to-go. As she hands me my order, I hear the cashier next to her wish another customer "Happy Mother's Day." It takes everything in me not to turn and tell her to fuck off. All around me are mothers and daughters dressed for morning church services or casually clothed for a day of shopping together. The smiles on their faces and the laughter in their voices brings my mood down another few notches and forces me to swallow past the lump in my throat. I want to hate all of them. Me, the person voted "Best Friend to Everyone" and "Most Likely to Succeed in Making Everyone Laugh" in high school wants to walk up to complete strangers in a bagel shop and throw my cloud of doom over them by reminding them to cherish what they have because one day they might not have it anymore. At some point, without any warning, it can be ripped right out of their hands in the blink of an eye.

As more and more Mother's Day greetings fill the air around me, I fight the urge to scream at everyone. I snatch the bag with the cinnamon bagel in it, grab the coffee cup from the counter, and curse loudly when some of the scalding hot liquid splashes out of the drinking hole in the lid and onto my hand.

With a glare at the happy, smiling patrons, I exit Panera Bread, get into my car, and make the dreaded fifteen-minute drive to the cemetery so I can spend Mother's Day with my mom, a cup of coffee, a bottle of pills, and a straightedge razor.

Chapter One
The First Cut is the Deepest

Ten months later.

"Have you thought about going to a support group, Addison? I really think speaking to others who are dealing with the same hardships as yourself would benefit you tremendously."

I stare, unblinking, at my therapist as she continues with her spiel. She reminds me so much of my mother that it almost takes my breath away. The first time I walked into her office, the smell of Venezia Perfume assaulted my senses, and I almost turned and ran out of the room. I've never known of anyone else to wear that perfume, except for one person. My doctor has the same hairstyle, the same sense of humor, and gives the same type of no-nonsense advice. I've been going to see her ever since I got out of the hospital, and at this point I think I'm a glutton for punishment. I don't want to be reminded of my mom week after week, and yet I can't stay away. I can't stop myself from wanting to be near someone who is so much like her.

"Here's a list of meetings in your area," she explains, handing me a sheet of paper with locations, dates, and times typed on them. "They say that you should go to at least six meetings before you make a decision on whether or not it's right for you. Give it a try. Open yourself up to people who understand what you're going through. I really think it will help. Don't make me start lecturing you because then you'll roll your eyes at me and I'll have to nag you until you finally give in."

"Lord, grant me the serenity to accept the things I cannot change, the courage to change the things I can, and the wisdom to know the difference. Keep coming back. It works if you work it with a lot of love!"

The cheerfulness makes me want to roll my eyes, but instead I bite the inside of my cheek just in case Dr. Thompson somehow found a way to keep her eyes on me. A circle of twenty or so people unclasp their hands after the end-of-meeting prayer and disperse to chitchat. I never understand how these people can smile and act normal after they just spent an hour telling the room their deep, dark secrets. Like Diane, the woman whose son overdosed on heroin this past weekend after he sold off all of her furniture and jewelry to support his habit. Or Mike, the young husband whose wife drove their two daughters to

5

school drunk, went left-of-center a mile from the school, and crashed into a telephone pole, killing the youngest daughter instantly.

Just as I've been doing for the past six weeks, I pick up my purse from the floor and walk out of the room with my head down, not speaking to anyone.

I'm not going to lie. When Dr. Thompson handed me the piece of paper with support group locations on it months ago, I crumbled it up and tossed it into my backseat as soon as I got in my car. After ten months of talking ad nauseam about why I'm not happy with my life, I'm pretty sure she thinks I'm a hopeless case and is just trying to pawn me off on someone else without making it too obvious. She's certain I've gotten over my "hump" and am no longer a threat to myself. Now, she wants me to lean on others for help with my father.

This is the sixth Al-Anon meeting I've been to in six weeks. I honestly can't tell you why I keep coming back. It doesn't "work if I work it" because I don't care to work it. I never share my story, I never make comments about anyone else's hardships, and I never make friends with any of the people I spend an hour with each week as they pour their hearts out to a room full of virtual strangers.

Except they aren't really strangers. They all know one another, share with each other, and lean on each other for support. *I* am the stranger in their midst. I am the weird girl who always sits just outside of the circle and chooses to "pass" when the conversation makes its way to her each week. I don't feel comfortable talking to people I *know* about my alcoholic father and how he's been in and out of rehab more times than I can count in the past year and a half, let alone talking to people who know nothing about me. I used to have no trouble talking to people, no matter who they were, about my problems. But that was a long time ago, and my problems usually consisted of what outfit to wear to school the next day or whether or not the boy I liked would ask me out. Things have changed a lot since then. I've put up walls and I've locked away all of my feelings because I've been crippled by the pain of being so alone, and I'm mistrustful of everyone around me. The people closest to me let me down and left me to fend for myself. How can I possibly trust *anyone* with my story and my feelings when I know that in the end, they'll just turn their back on me? They always do.

I make my way down to the first floor of Metro Hospital and out the front doors into the crisp night air, taking a few deep breaths as I walk to my car in the parking lot. Every week it's the same thing. I feel panic bubbling up in my throat as I listen to everyone's discussions, and I nervously tap my foot on the floor, counting down the minutes on the clock hanging on the wall until it's time to leave.

I still have no idea what forces me to return each week; no clue what possesses me to get in my car at 7:45pm every Tuesday night and drive the couple of blocks to the hospital and go up to the fifteenth floor to the meeting room. I'm not getting anything out of these meetings. I haven't learned how to "let go and let God" or "fake it till you make it" or any of those other crap slogans they stole from Alcoholics Anonymous.

I have a father who shut himself off from life the day my mother died and chose to console himself at the bottom of a bottle of vodka on a daily basis. I was dealing with the loss of my best friend while making sure my father didn't choke on his own vomit or die from alcohol poisoning. I was a senior in high school with my whole life ahead of me, and I had to check my father into his first stint in rehab a month after the funeral, take on the role of administrator for my mother's estate, and learn how to run a business—all in one day. I was suddenly the parent instead of the child. Up until that point, I was in the National Honor Society and slated for Valedictorian. After we buried her, I was lucky I even graduated.

All of the grief and heartache and responsibilities turned me into a person I barely recognized. One day my mother was here, doling out advice and helping me through life, and the next day she was gone. No warning, no heads up—just gone. Her life was snuffed out like the flame on a birthday candle, without the wish. There was only darkness. The woman who kept our small family together and our lives running smoothly had suddenly disappeared, and I was left floundering on my own.

I pull out of the busy hospital parking lot, swearing to myself for the hundredth time that I won't go to next week's meeting. I make my way across town and pull around back of

Snow's Sugary Sweets—my mother's dream and my nightmare all rolled into one.

For years my mother made the desserts for every single wedding, graduation, baby shower, and family get-together. If she wasn't at work or out shopping, her second favorite pastime, she was in the kitchen baking. The house always smelled like butter and sugar and the oven was rarely off. Every time she showed up at an event with a tray full of goodies, people would tell her that she should just quit her job and open a bakery.

"Deena, these cookies are the best things I've ever eaten. What are they called and how do I make them?"

My mother let out a small chuckle as my aunt shoveled as many of the light, buttery confections in her mouth as she could handle.

"Those are called Lady Locks, Katie. They're very hard to make. I could give you the recipe, but then I'd have to kill you," she replied with a sinister laugh and a wag of her eyebrows.

"Fine, don't tell me. Just make sure you bring them to Christmas, Easter, my birthday, the kids' weddings, and any other get-together we have from now until we die. Or just open your own business already so I can come in every day and eat my weight in these things," my aunt stated seriously.

"Deal," my mom replied with a wink.

She laughed off the idea for a few years until she got laid off from her accounting job at a construction company when I was in junior high. With nothing to do day-in and day-out but wait for my father to wake up after sleeping the day away from working the night shift or for me to come home from school, she baked and started researching how to start your own business. Within two years, Snow's Sugary Sweets was up and running. Since our last name was Snow, it made choosing the name of the store easy. The hard part was getting my father on board with the plan.

"A bakery? We're opening a bakery?" my father asked in shock as he watched my mom hustle around the kitchen taking trays out of the oven, flicking switches on the four mixers she had going, and flipping through multiple recipe books.

"Yes, we're opening a bakery. Don't give me that look. You won't have to do anything other than tell me how amazing I am and be my taste tester," she reassured him as he rolled his eyes and heaved out a great big sigh. *"Think of it this way. If it does well, you'll be able to retire early and tell all of those idiots who take advantage of you at the*

mill where to stick it. Then we can pay someone else to do all the hard work, and we can travel like we always planned."

With just a few carefully crafted words from her, my father's fears were instantly soothed. She knew he was concerned about the amount of time she would spend away from him and the house. My parents were connected at the hip. Where one would go, the other would surely follow. They met in high school and were best friends until they both decided they wanted more. Their marriage was something I always envied: high school sweethearts who stood the test of time. They were the epitome of soul mates. They had their share of problems over the years, but when your love was built on friendship, you could come out stronger on the other side of any disagreement. My father's reaction to the bakery was the closest thing to an argument I had ever witnessed. He was scared that if my mother put all of her time and love into this business, there would be nothing left over for him. If he had learned anything over the years, though, it was to never argue with my mother. If she wanted something, she got it or she made it happen. My mother was a genius at making my father feel included and letting him make important decisions regarding the shop so he wouldn't feel like this was just her dream coming true, but one they could share together.

Snow's Sugary Sweets quickly became the talk of our small town. It was the only bakery within a twenty-mile radius, unless you wanted to go to Wal-Mart and choke down one of their dry cakes with greasy frosting that left a nasty, oily residue in your mouth after just one bite. It also helped that everyone loved my mother. She was sweet, friendly, and would do anything to help someone out. She had more friends than I could ever imagine having, and she was the reason Snow's became such a huge success.

As I use my keys to unlock the backdoor of the shop, I think about the love/hate relationship I have with the place. On one hand, I love that everything about this place reminds me of my mother, from the smell to the snowman décor that decorates the walls and counter tops year-round to tie in the "snow" part of the store name. On the other hand, I hate that everything about this place reminds me of my mother. I hate that everywhere I look I can't escape the memories.

"You're seriously going to put all of your snowmen decorations up at the bakery?" I asked my mom in shock as she pulled another blue tote off of the shelves in the basement where she had stored all of her holiday decorations. The snowmen always made an appearance as soon as Christmas was over. The tree and stockings would come down and

the snow globes, crystal snowflakes, and Snowbabies figurines would come out.

"Of course I'm going to put the snowmen up. They're adorable," she stated as she popped the lid off a tote and looked inside. Satisfied with what she found, she slid the tote next to the ten others currently taking up most of the floor space in the back corner of the basement.

"But it's July. In Ohio. Don't you think that's a little weird?"

My mom pulled a stuffed snowman out of a tote who, when a button was pushed on its hand, would dance to the tune of Ice Ice Baby that blasted out of a speaker in its ass.

"Who in their right mind would think snowmen are weird?" she asked as she bobbed her head and shuffled her feet to Vanilla Ice.

"Um, me," I stated.

"Well, you're a teenager. You think everything is weird. And you dress funny, so really, you have no say in the matter. I blame you anyway. You're the one who started buying snowmen for me."

"Hey, it's not my fault the Secret Santa shop at school sucks. And I was nine. You can't hold that against me," I complained as I got down on my knees and started looking through one of the open totes.

"Oh yes I can. That's the joy of being a mother. I can blame you for whatever I want because I'm the adult," she said with a laugh.

"I can't wait to have my own kids so I can torture them like you do me," I told her as I pulled a snow globe out and held it up in front of me, watching the snow swirl gently around the snowman inside.

"Oh believe me, I can't wait until you have kids either. I curse you with a daughter just like you so you can feel my pain and I can sit back, point, and laugh."

A sharp pain shoots through my chest when I remember how many times my mother and I had that same conversation about children. According to her, I was a monster as a baby. I never slept through the night, I had colic, and I was just an all-around pain in the ass. This of course only intensified when I became a teenager with PMS. She delighted in the fact that one day she would get to watch me live through the same hell with my own children. But that would never be. She would never coach me through childbirth or give me advice on what type of food to serve at a first birthday party. None of that matters now since I'm never going to have children. It's hard enough living day in and day out without her; I can't even imagine the pain of doing it with children who will never meet their grandmother.

I immediately shut off my mind from the memories. I can't think about her. If I do, I'll fall back down the rabbit hole and never be able to surface. I know it's not healthy to use this on/off switch as much as I do, but it's the only way I know how to survive. The only way I can wake up each day, put one foot in front of the other, and keep going.

With a sigh, I flip on the light switch in the kitchen and get to work preparing the dough for the next day's cookies and the batter for the cupcakes. While I mix and stir, I think about the holiday coming up next month and wonder if my dad, on his fifth trip to rehab, will still be sober when that date rolls around. I feel a moment of shame when I remember that day at the cemetery. After ten months of therapy, I still can't say the words out loud to anyone. My therapist tries over and over to get me to relive that day's events, but I refuse. Instead, we talk about coping, living your life to the fullest, and how to overcome the grief that can swallow you whole. I put on a good show of acting like I'm "cured" and that I'm ready to join the land of the living. I prove to her that I'm better and that thoughts of death and darkness don't consume my every thought anymore.

She will never be privy to my dreams at night, though, and she will never know how many times I still wonder if I would be happier away from this place, away from the pain and despair of trying to go on with my life when the most important person in my world is no longer there to help me.

As I crack an egg into the big mixing bowl, the faint, jagged scar on the inside of my left wrist gives me pause and brings the memories I hate to think about, but ones that will never leave me alone, swirling to the surface.

"Hi-ya mmo-om," I slurred as I plopped down on top of the dirt below her headstone and crisscrossed my legs. The handful of pills I swallowed with a sip of coffee on the drive over were starting to work their magic. I felt like I was floating on a cloud, and the thoughts in my head were fuzzy.

I stared at the small, oval circle below her name that held a picture of her at my cousin's wedding the previous October. I hated headstones that had pictures on them. I hated that this was the one we picked out. And of course by "we" I meant me. My father was too busy taste-testing different flavors of vodka that day to pick out anything, and two hours after the funeral, our extended families all went back to the comfort of their own homes and forgot about the grieving people they left behind to suffer and struggle. They went back to their happy homes and their happy lives, and life just went on for them. The moment they walked out of the church, the cloud of death lifted from their shoulders, and they were able to fold up the sadness and put it in a back pocket and never think about it again while we were stuck trying to figure out how to cope and breathe again.

"Happy Mother'sssssday," I mumbled as I popped the lid off of her cup of hazelnut coffee and poured it slowly into the dirt in front of me, watching it quickly disappear into the dry ground.

When the cup was empty, I put the lid back on and set it down next to me, reaching for the bag with the bagel in it. I had to widen my eyes and blink a few times to get the bag to come into focus so I could open it and remove the cinnamon crunch bagel. I set it down right on top of the headstone and let out a huge sigh.

"I can't do this without you. I hate that you're not here. I hate it so much," I said to the picture on the headstone, trying in vain to keep the tears at bay. They rolled down my cheeks on their own volition and dropped onto my knees.

I picked at a few stray blades of grass that had popped up around the disturbed earth and began breaking little pieces off while the tears continued to fall.

"What am I supposed to do without you? How the hell am I supposed to do this?" I cried angrily.

I fiddled with a few more pieces of grass and wiped my nose on the back of my hand, the words on the headstone and my mother's picture beginning to blur and swirl in front of my eyes.

"I don't want to be here without you. I don't know how...I don't know how to live without you here."

A soft breeze blew through the trees, and I lifted my face up toward the sky and let it caress me, hoping that maybe it was a sign from her that she wanted me to do this, that she wanted me with her. With my eyes still closed, I reached into the front pocket of my shorts and removed the razor, lightly running my thumb back and forth over the top, thinking about how sleepy I was and how easy it would be to just curl up on top of the dirt and take a nap.

Without opening my eyes, I brought the razor to the inside of my wrist and made the first cut.

Chapter Two

Over You

"How are things with your father?" Dr. Thompson asks.

Her office is bright and airy, and at the start of every meeting, she apologizes and then gets up to shut the blinds, covering the window above her desk so the sun doesn't blind either of us. She always makes a joke about wanting to blind me so I'll forget I'm in a doctor's office and it will trick me into opening up to her more. Every time she says it I wonder if she knew my mother in another life and stole all of her best lines.

I always sit on the buttery soft, white leather couch with my shoes off and my legs curled up underneath me, and Dr. Thompson sits directly across from me in a dark blue recliner. She says it's more comfortable and inviting to talk this way, and she hopes it makes people feel like they're just chatting in her living room. Her office is warm and inviting, which I guess is typical of a therapist's office. I wouldn't know since she's the only one I've ever been to. I always find myself staring at a Thomas Kinkaid painting of a snowy cottage scene on Christmas Eve that hangs on the wall. My parents used to have the exact same painting above their fireplace until my dad removed all traces of my mother the day after she died. I wonder where that painting is now.

"Okay I guess. He always manages to call at the most inopportune times and then gets frustrated when I don't have time to talk. He has no clue how busy I am or that everything doesn't revolve around his stupid drinking problem."

I say this quickly and try to gloss over the importance of those words and what they do to me when I speak them aloud. Dr. Thompson isn't going to be fooled though.

"This is his fifth time in rehab, correct?"

I nod in response, the reality of just how different my life is from a year and a half ago glaringly obvious.

"How do you feel about the fact that he wasn't able to stay sober all those times when he got out?" she asks as she folds her hands in her lap on top of the pad of paper with the pencil sticking up between her fingers.

"Hurt. Sad. Pissed off."

"Your mother's death hit him hard," she states.

"It hit both of us hard. It was unexpected and it shouldn't have happened like it did. I needed him and he wasn't there for me."

Dr. Thompson unclasps her hands and writes a few things on the paper.

"Do you blame your father for your suicide attempt?"

I cringe when she says the word *suicide*. I don't want to be placed in this category of weak people who have nothing left to live for and feel like it's their only way out. After all of the soul searching I've been forced to do since that day at the cemetery, I've realized I don't really want to die. I just want to feel something other than sadness. Even though I question God every day, and no longer believe in half the things I was taught growing up in the Catholic Church, one thing still remains with me. If I took my own life, heaven—if there even is such a place—is not where I would wind up.

"Yes. No. I don't know, maybe." I sigh irritably in response to her question. "He crumbled when she died. Just...faded away. It was like I lost both parents in one day. It was too much."

"I think you have every right to be disappointed in him for his actions. You just need to remember that he's grieving too. He lost his wife and he'll never get her back," Dr. Thompson says softly.

"And I lost my mother. At least he can move on someday and find another wife. I'll never have another mom."

"Meg, can you grab me a dozen of the devil's food cupcakes with the cream cheese frosting from the back, please?" I yell to Snow's other employee as she disappears through the swinging door behind the counter while I ring up a customer.

Meg's twenty-two, bubbly, and outgoing—the complete opposite as me, but she reminds me so much of my old self that I was instantly drawn to her. I had met her during my mandatory seventy-two hour psych evaluation at Metro Hospital. I still will never understand how someone like her wound up in a place like a psych ward, which just shows how out of touch I was with my own mental health. We met just outside the hospital two hours after I woke up from my sedation when I was permitted five minutes of supervised fresh air.

"White is obviously not a good color for us. My name's Meg."

She pointed to the white gauze secured around my wrist and then held up her own wrapped arm.

"We're like the Wonder Twins. Powers activate!"

She bumped her wrist against my own and made the sound of an explosion when she moved hers away then plopped down on the bench next to me.

"Too bad they don't have pink to match my slippers," she said dejectedly as we both look down at the fuzzy bunny slippers on her feet.

Meg and I were in separate therapy groups while we were there, so I never found out what the cause of her suicide attempt was, which I guess is a good thing because that means she doesn't know my secrets either. It's easy to be friends with someone who doesn't know about the demons chasing you.

On the day I was released, I saw Meg again outside smoking a cigarette while I waited for a taxi to take me home. I bummed one off of her, even though I don't smoke, because she looked like she needed some company.

As I took a drag of my first cigarette, the smoke filled my lungs too quickly and I began heaving and coughing so hard I thought I would throw up.

"Jesus, did Bill Clinton teach you nothing? Don't inhale, dude," Meg said with a laugh as she took the cigarette from my hand and pitched it over into the grass.

"You heading out of here today, too?" she asked when I finally managed to stop hacking up a lung.

"Yep. Just got my walking papers and a long list of therapists I'm supposed to call as soon as I get home," I told her as she grabbed the list from my hands and skimmed through it.

"Judgmental, too old, chronic halitosis, don't know that one, this one tried to get in my pants...ooooooh that one is nice," Meg stated as she read each name on my list. "I think the Wonder Twins should pick that one."

I leaned over her shoulder to see who she pointed to.

"I went to her a few years ago but had to stop when my dad's insurance changed. Now that I have no job and no real direction in life, the state pays for my insurance so I can go to whomever I want," she stated matter-of-factly.

"Do you need a job?"

Meg shrugged as she folded up the page of therapist names and handed it back to me. "Money would be nice. I used to work at a daycare, but they sent me an email yesterday telling me that I'm no longer good role model material for the children. Um, hello? Suicidal here! That could have totally pushed me over the edge and they don't even care," Meg said dramatically.

I didn't even hesitate before offering her a job at the bakery. Meg makes me smile and she doesn't try to pry into my life. Aside from the day she told me she lost her job, neither one of us has shared anything more personal with each other. Out of necessity, I had to tell her my father was "occupied elsewhere" since technically he still owns the business. She doesn't know that this is his fifth time in rehab or the cause for his spiral out of control. She doesn't know that I planned on graduating from high school, fully intent on going to college to become a writer, and I hate my father a little more each day for forcing me to take on the responsibilities that should have been his instead of doing something about my own dreams and aspirations. Meg knows enough to not ask questions. It's the reason why we get along so well.

Weekdays after school lets out are always busy days at Snow's. The best part about the shop is that it's enjoyed by young and old alike. A group of high school students can be seen sharing a table with a married couple from the retirement home around the corner. A mother and her newborn baby often chat and receive advice from a couple whose son just went off to college. Today is a teacher in-service day at the high school and it seems like the entire four grade levels of students and teachers have been shuffling in and out of the shop since we opened at seven o'clock this morning.

Since I was a freshman in high school when my mother opened the store, I had made the place a teenage hangout from day one. My friends thought it was the best thing in the world that my mom would give us free snacks after school every day and let us pretend we were cool by allowing us a cup of coffee to sip on in the mornings. My mom was always known as the "cool" parent with all my friends, even before she owned the bakery and the lure of chocolate and cake seduced every teenager within a mile radius. My mom was the type of parent who would let me have parties every weekend after the Friday night football games and allowed my friends to drink a few beers as long as they gave her their car keys and spent the night on the living room floor. My mom was the one who never gave me a curfew and, instead, trusted me to make the right decisions and call her if I was ever in trouble. My friends all envied me, but I never fully appreciated how awesome she was until I got older.

"Hey, who's the hottie that keeps checking you out?" Meg asks as she comes back out of the kitchen with a tray of cupcakes.

I hand a customer her change and nonchalantly glance over to the corner of the shop where Meg is looking. My eyes connect with the most piercing blue eyes I've ever seen, and a tingle runs down my spine. His eyes never leave mine—not to check out the rest of me like most guys do, nor to look anywhere else around the room even though chaos surrounds him. I watch his eyes soften and the corner of his mouth start to turn up into a smile. I feel butterflies in my stomach that I haven't felt in forever and quickly break the eye contact when I see that he has no intention of doing so. His blatant staring makes me uncomfortable, like he's trying to see inside me and find out what makes me tick. I don't need anyone knowing that much about me, especially a stranger.

"I have no idea. Never seen him before," I tell her, the lie slipping easily off my tongue. He's a stranger, that much is true, but I've seen him before. I've seen him sit at the same table in the corner of the room once a week for the past few months. I've heard the deep melodic notes of his voice when he orders a chocolate scone and black coffee— two sugars—each and every time he's here. I don't know how I remember what his order is. We have hundreds of customers and it's not like I remember all of their orders. The first day he came into the shop, I felt a jolt of recognition when he came up to the counter, a sense of déjà vu, like I had seen this guy before in another time. I waited for him to say something about knowing me from somewhere as I rang up his order, but he never did. He thanked me with a nod of his head and a smile, never saying more to me than what his order was each week.

"Well, whoever he is, he's yummy. And I've caught him checking you out the entire hour he's been here nursing that coffee," Meg says as she pushes the tray of cupcakes into the display case under the front counter.

"He can look all he wants as long as he keeps his distance."

Meg turns to face me and places her hands on either side of my face. "How do you expect to get laid if you make everyone keep their distance?" she asks with mock seriousness.

"Um, maybe by not *expecting* to get laid. I barely have time to shave my legs or take a shower anymore. I'm not in the market for a guy."

The store phone rings, saving me from having yet another discussion with Meg on why I don't have a boyfriend.

Even if I *did* want someone in my life just to scratch an itch, they would always want more. More information, more history, more answers to questions I wouldn't give— more of *me* that I stopped giving away a year and a half ago.

Meg answers the phone and immediately hands the receiver out to me. "It's your dad."

The tone in her voice is sympathetic. My dad always seems to call when she's around, and she's gotten her fill of the one-sided conversations, enough to know that my father and I aren't on the best terms.

"Hey, hon," my dad greets happily when I take the phone. "How are things?"

"Busy," I state curtly.

"Any big party orders coming up this week?" he asks, attempting to make conversation.

"Nope."

I can tell my one-word answers frustrate him by the huge sigh he lets out on his end of the line. He spends day in and day out learning how to communicate with his loved ones and how to live a healthy life. He expects me to jump right on board with him and pour out my heart, but I've done that before and got nothing in return. Fool me once, shame on you, fool me twice…

"Yeah, I'm busy here too. Just got out of group session. I've got some homework to do tonight. Need to make a list of all the people I've wronged while I was using. I think I'll probably need more than one night," he says with a laugh.

I don't return his amusement.

I'm not a cruel person. I was one-hundred-percent supportive of my father the first time he went into rehab. He would call several times a day, whenever he had a free minute, and I encouraged him and asked questions and supported his sobriety every way I could. I was proud of him for making the decision that he needed help and for being the one to make that difficult phone call asking for it. I believed every single word that came out of his mouth during those thirty days. I believed he was sorry, that he loved me, that he knew he screwed up, and that he would do everything in his power to remain sober and be a solid support system for me. I visited him every single Saturday during Family Day, the one day a week when they were allowed visitors, and I participated in every "Smack Down Sunday" where loved ones got to tell their addict just how hurt they were by their actions. After his third, failed stint in rehab, my support went out the window with his sobriety.

I learned a very valuable lesson at that point in time and it is this: how can you tell if an addict is lying? He opens his mouth.

"So, I was wondering if you were planning on coming up to Family Day this weekend. I need to let my counselor know so she can get you a visitor's pass."

I walk away as far as the cord will allow so Meg and the customers can't hear me.

"I wasn't planning on it. I've got a lot going on here right now," I tell him, turning my back to the customers and resting my forehead against the wall.

"Well, I really want to see you," he replies earnestly.

"Yeah, I get that. But I just don't have the time. I'm sorry."

He sighs into the phone again, and I know I've made him angry.

"Seriously, Addison. You haven't been to one single Family Day since I've been here. I'm the only one in my group who never gets any visitors," he complains.

I feel the anger bubbling up inside me, and it takes everything in me not to scream into the phone.

"Dad, it's an hour and a half drive one way. Weekends are the busiest times at the shop. I can't be away that long. You know that."

"You know what? Forget it. Forget I even asked. I'll talk to you later."

The dial tone sounds in my ear before I can even reply. I roll my eyes and walk back to hang up the phone.

My dad is like Jekyll and Hyde. For the most part, when he's clean and sober he reminds me of the man he used to be when my mother was alive—easy going, funny, always helping people out, and hard working. When he's drinking, he turns into a cruel person who lashes out with hateful words and spiteful accusations. Even with all of the therapy he's received, it still hasn't sunk in that all of those words have left their mark on me.

Each one sliced into me and took a chunk out of my heart. It's easy to forgive someone for the hurt they've caused you. Forgetting is impossible.

"What the hell do you want from me?" my dad yelled.

The smell of whiskey leaking from his pores nauseated me. It was the Fourth of July and I made an appearance at a family cookout even though my heart wasn't in it. He'd been out of rehab for two weeks. Fourteen days was as long as he lasted this time. It was a new record. Last time it was nine.

As far as I knew, he wasn't coming today. One of the biggest drinking and partying days of the year, next to New Year's Eve, probably wasn't the best idea for a recovering alcoholic, but he showed up anyway. He pulled into the driveway, and as soon as he got out of the car I knew. I could tell by the way he walked, the way he held himself, and the way he spoke loudly to everyone around him. I tried to avoid him. I knew if I got within two feet of him, we'd exchange words and they wouldn't be pleasant ones. When he was drunk, I didn't have any patience for him and he hated everything about me.

Even though I knew I would regret it, he asked to speak with me privately. I relented, walking over to the side of the house where he waited for me. It only took five minutes of him pleading with me about what he could do to make things better between us before the talk turned ugly.

"How about staying sober for once. That would be a good start. I'm sick and tired of taking care of everything."

He scoffed and rolled his eyes at me. "Oh poor you. For once in your pampered life you actually have to lift a finger and get off of your lazy ass."

His words cut into me like a knife and choked the breath from my lungs. I should be used to the sting of them by now, but I wasn't. I should have learned that there was no use in arguing with a drunk, but I hadn't. I turned and walked away from him, knowing that separating myself from him was the only option at this point. Nothing I said to him would break through the haze of alcohol that had taken hold of his brain and his ability to think clearly.

"Oh that's right. Walk away. It's what you do best. You are such a bitch!"

Meg bumps her shoulder into mine and pulls my thoughts away from the past.

"Hey, that guy that was checking you out left you a note," Meg tells me with a huge smile on her face as I turn around and shut off my switch. She hands me a folded up napkin as I glance to the back corner table that is now empty. I open it and in neat, block letters are the words:

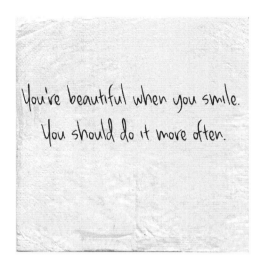

You're beautiful when you smile.
You should do it more often.

I laugh uncomfortably and push the note back at her. "I doubt that's for me. I'm sure he meant you."

Meg glances at the words and then rolls her eyes. She thrusts the note back at me. "Oh please! He didn't even give me a second glance. He only had eyes for you. That guy is the sweetest ever. And you really are beautiful when you smile."

She bats her eyelashes at me, and I lightly smack her in the arm before she makes a big deal about something that clearly isn't. Meg walks away laughing, and I shake my head at her back. I crumple up the napkin, shove it into my pocket, and get back to work, trying to forget about the cute guy in the corner and why in the world he would ever leave me a note.

I finally get home from work at ten o'clock that evening, take a quick shower to wash the cake batter off of my skin, and sit down at the desk in my room. I power up my computer and open Facebook, automatically going to her page. I start a new private message to her, just like I do every single night before I go to bed. I know I should have deleted her profile ages ago, but I could never bring myself to do it. Obviously nothing about what I do is healthy, but I don't care. Every time I would hover my mouse over the settings of her page to delete it, my chest would tighten and I would struggle to breathe. Deleting it seems wrong. It would be like deleting her from my life. As much as I hate to think about her, I'm not ready to do that yet. Taking a deep breath and pushing past the pain, I type my post.

Dear Mom,
I miss you. I wish you were here.
I miss you more today than yesterday,
but not half as much as tomorrow.
Love,
Addison

Chapter Three
Stubborn Love

"Why do you hate going to the meetings so much, Addison?" Dr. Thompson asks as I settle in on the couch and notice a cup of coffee from Panera sitting on her side table. I close my eyes for a moment and pretend like I'm speaking to my mother while she sips her favorite coffee.

"I just think they're pointless. It's not like I'm getting anything out of them."

She cocks her head and smiles at me.

"And yet you keep going back. You keep going back to the same place, week after week, with the same people. I know it's hard for you to go back to that hospital, the place you spent so much time while your mother was sick, but you still do it. Why do you think that is?"

She sits there patiently, waiting for me to answer her, but I don't have an answer. I honestly don't know why I continue to go back.

"Even though you won't admit it, I think going to these meetings gives you comfort. It makes you feel a little more normal because you know you aren't the only one struggling with someone who has an addiction. You aren't as alone as you think you are, Addison. Around every corner is a possibility: a possibility of hope, of friendship, of support. This week, try and put yourself out there. Tell them your name, open up to them, give them *something*. Show them who you are and don't be afraid. No one can help you, no one WILL help you, if you won't let them. For God's sakes, let them help you so I can stop giving you these boring lectures."

She punctuates her statement with a short, loud laugh exactly like my mother's. For a moment, it's easy to imagine *her* sitting across from me instead of Dr. Thompson. I would have immediately taken her advice without a second though had it been my mother doling out words of wisdom.

I pull into the parking lot of the hospital at quarter past eight in the evening and have to wait another ten minutes for an elevator. Regardless of the fact that I absolutely hate these meetings, I hate the fact that they have to be *here*—the same place where I spent the better part of my last two years of high school. I hate the smells, I hate the sights, and I hate that I continue to come here week after week and subject myself to this torture.

At 7:50 I was adamant that I wasn't going to another meeting since it was pointless to keep going to something that clearly wasn't helping me at all.

At 8:00 I was starting up my car and cursing loudly as I backed out of the driveway of my apartment.

The elevator takes its sweet time going up and stops on almost every floor. I let out a growl of frustration as it stops on the seventh floor and my eyes pop out of my head when I see who gets on.

What the hell is HE doing here?

It's the guy from the coffee shop. The one I pretend to never notice but think about constantly. The one who always smiles at me and who wrote me a note on a napkin. A napkin I swore I would throw away, but now it sits next to my laptop at home, smoothed out from the irritated crumple I gave it.

His footsteps falter as our eyes meet, but he quickly recovers and smiles broadly at me as he gets on and stands right next to me.

"Ten, please," he happily tells the woman standing directly in front of the elevator buttons as he shifts his backpack up a little higher on the shoulder he has it slung over. I stare straight ahead at the closing doors, wishing I could make my feet move to run out of there. I refuse to look at "Napkin Guy" even though I can see him staring down at me out of the corner of my eye.

The elevator crawls up to the next floor and dings its arrival before the doors open again. I silently curse the person who gets on and stands right in front of me, blocking my escape.

"Fancy meeting you here, Bakery Girl," he finally whispers to me in the crowded elevator.

Bakery Girl? Did he just call me Bakery Girl?

I grind my teeth and finally turn to face him, my breath catching in my throat when I see how close his face is to mine. He's about a head taller than me, and he bends down so he can speak without being overheard. I've always noticed how cute he was from a few feet away at the bakery, but being this close to him is distracting.

"Are you stalking me?" I whisper angrily, saying the first thing that comes to my jumbled mind.

His smile immediately broadens and he chuckles to himself as he moves in even closer and speaks right next to my ear, his chest brushing up against my arm.

"If I was, this would be the most boring and depressing place for me to show off my mad stalking skills. This place is sick. Literally."

The clean, manly smell of his cologne is disrupting my concentration, and his nearness and joking manner make me feel nervous. Aside from Meg, people don't joke around with me anymore. Lately, I don't really have the type of personality that begs to be played with or teased in any way.

I take a step away from him, forcing me to bump up against the nurse in purple hospital scrubs on the other side of me.

I hear him chuckle under his breath again as I turn my body away from him and pretend like I am completely engrossed in watching the numbers above the door light up for each floor they pass.

"Are you visiting someone?" he whispers, close to me again.

Jesus, he's like a ninja.

I keep my face straight-ahead and don't acknowledge his question.

"You're not sick, are you? Maybe I shouldn't stand so close. You might be contagious."

His jovial demeanor makes me want to look him straight in the eye and tell him that I am indeed sick, but luckily for him, it's nothing he can catch. He's obviously not going to stop until I give him something. Maybe if I'm mean enough, he'll go away.

"The Stalkers Anonymous meeting is on the second floor. I think you made a wrong turn, Napkin Guy," I mutter angrily without looking at him.

"Did you just call me *Napkin Guy*?" he asks with a laugh. "My name's actually Zander. And Stalkers Anonymous is on the fourth floor, and they only meet on days when the person they're stalking is busy or when Creepers Consortium is cancelled."

As more people get on and off the slowest elevator known to man, I continue to ignore him, even though it's growing increasingly painful to keep biting my lip to stop myself from smiling at his quick comebacks. When the doors take too long to close after the last person exits, he reaches in front of me and hits the "close doors" button, his arm brushing up against me, and I have to force myself not to shiver.

I glance at him out of the corner of my eye while he stares straight-ahead and hums along to the muzak version of *Stairway to Heaven* that's being piped through the speakers in the elevator. He looks to be in his early twenties. He's got short, black hair that appears to have been freshly cut by how clean the lines are at the edge of his neck and around his sideburns. He wets his lips with his tongue, and when I manage to tear my gaze away from those lips, I realize he's staring at me again and has caught me practically drooling while watching him. I quickly turn my eyes away and feel a blush form on my cheeks.

I don't know what he's doing here, and I wasn't really joking when I called him a stalker. While I should probably be nervous that he seems to be following me around, there's something about him that puts me at ease. I've kept myself closed off from people for so long that the feeling of my heart rate quickening in excitement instead of dread is a strange sensation. It should make me happy that *something* has the ability to do that to me, but all it does is irritate me. I don't need some weird guy trying to get in my pants, which I'm sure that's what this is about. Or he's just a friendly person who will talk to anyone no matter where he is, just like my mother.

"I've been lucky. I haven't had any nausea at all with the chemo. My sister had breast cancer about ten years ago and it was horrible for her. She would throw up for days afterward. My doctor still gave me a prescription for Zofran just in case."

I walked up behind my mom who was in a deep discussion with the cashier at Macy's. I pulled my cell phone out of my purse and started scrolling through texts to distract myself from the topic of my mom's cancer. She was having a good day, and I didn't want anything to ruin it, especially my worries.

"Make sure you tell Dr. Fuller I said hello. She was wonderful. I still get a Christmas card from her every year," the cashier told my mother as she slid the receipt into her bag and lifted it over the counter to her.

"I will, Debbie. I'll also tell her about your new granddaughter."

"That would be wonderful. Take care and I will make sure to keep you in my prayers," Debbie, the cashier, said with a kind smile on her face.

My mom said good-bye and we made our way out of Macy's and head towards the food court for lunch.

"Where do you know that Debbie person from?"

My mom looked over at me and shrugged. "I don't. I just met her."

The elevator stops on Zander's floor before I realize it, and I quickly dig through my purse looking for my phone to busy myself before he tries to engage me in more conversation or God forbid ask me out. It's not until the elevator doors are closing behind him, and I'm still pawing through my purse, that I look up and realize he didn't even look my way or make an attempt to talk to me again before he got off. I don't realize how much I actually *wanted* him to do something like that until I feel a twinge of disappointment as he walks away from me.

"See you around, Bakery Girl," he says over his shoulder as I watch the doors close and feel the elevator start to move again with my mouth wide open.

I'm distracted.

My mind is a jumbled mess ever since Zander walked away from me in the elevator almost two weeks ago. I've burnt cupcakes, dropped entire trays of cookies, and snapped at Meg, which I never do. She's the nicest person in the world, who doesn't look at me with pity, and I bit her head off about an order that *I* wrote down wrong.

I skip the following week's meeting, not wanting to chance running into Zander again with his easy laugh or pretty eyes or the way he completely shocked me by just walking away. Even though I hate those damn meetings, I feel uneasy after missing one. I keep checking to make sure I don't leave the oven on, and I keep patting my pockets to make sure I still have my car keys. After running back into the apartment this morning to make sure I unplugged the iron, I kicked the front tire of my car when I got back outside, frustrated that all of this nonsense is over me feeling guilty about skipping a stupid meeting—a meeting that never helped me and never made a difference in my life.

My frustration is the only explanation as to why I am currently stalking over to the table in the corner—the table where Zander currently sits reading the paper. It's the same table where I found six more notes that followed in the first one's wake, each one reminding me that I'm much more beautiful when I smile or trying to fool me with humor like yesterday's note. *"Every time you frown, God kills a kitten."* I should have known that skipping the meeting wouldn't just make him disappear. And of course Meg has been having a field day over those stupid napkin notes, telling me that it's something right out of a Hallmark made-for-television movie.

Who the hell does he think he is?

"Who the hell do you think you are?" I ask angrily as I stop right next to his table and fold my arms protectively across my chest.

43

He glances up from his paper and my breath catches in my throat. I was too distracted a few weeks ago by the fact that he was at *my* hospital in *my* personal space to notice anything other than how good he smelled or that he was cute. Staring at him now, I notice that his eyes aren't just blue. They're crystal blue. They sparkle as the sun shines in from the window next to him, and incredibly long, dark lashes frame them.

One side of his mouth turns up in a smile, and a dimple I never noticed before pops up out of nowhere on the lower part of his left cheek. His jaw is smooth and freshly shaven, and he has a small scar above his right eyebrow that I have an unnatural urge to run my finger over. I'm so busy blatantly staring that I momentarily forget my purpose for coming over to his table. My eyes are taking in his soft, full lips, and after a few seconds of ogling them, I realize they are moving and he's answering my demanded question.

"I think I already established in the elevator that I'm Zander, but I could be wrong. You sound really pissed, so how about you just tell me who I am," he says me with a grin.

"I don't care what your stupid name is. I care about why you keep leaving me these annoying notes." Ignoring that stupid dimple, I smack the handful of stupid napkins with the stupid messages on them on top of the stupid table in front of him. His coffee cup rattles against the table with the force of my hand, and he glances back and forth from the pile of napkins to my face.

"You kept all of my notes?" he asks softly, his eyebrows rising in shock.

Seriously? That's the only thing he has to say?

"Stop leaving me notes. Stop staring at me. And stop smiling," I growl before turning on my heels and walking away.

"Is it okay if I still breathe? What about blink? Is blinking allowed, Bakery Girl?" he calls to my back.

"Stop calling me Bakery Girl. My name is ADDISON!" I shout in irritation over my shoulder as I round the corner of the counter and walk past a smiling Meg resting her elbows on the counter with her chin in her hands. She opens her mouth to speak, and I hold up my hand in front of her face.

"Don't. Not one word," I warn her before I keep going, slamming both of my hands into the swinging door that leads to the back room.

I start dragging mixing bowls and pots and pans down from the cupboards, banging them onto the counter and cursing at myself as I go.

What in the hell possessed me to talk to him? He's going to be like a stray cat that you feel sorry for and feed out on your front porch. I'm never going to be able to get rid of him now.

I grow increasingly angrier at myself when I realize that I'm not exactly sure if I'm happy or pissed that he might keep coming back, and I wonder if Dr. Thompson will be pleased that I showed him who I was AND told him my name. It's probably not exactly what she had in mind when she told me to share part of myself with someone, but I don't really care. Now he knows I'm a bitch, and if he's smart, he'll change his mind and won't want anything more to do with me.

Chapter Four

Just Breathe

"When was the last time you did something just for you? Something that made you happy and had nothing to do with anyone else?" Dr. Thompson asks as I curl up in my usual position on her pristine white couch. She stares at me and then twitches her nose like Samantha on the old television show *Bewitched*. My mother had the same facial tick. We used to joke with her that it wasn't something she did unconsciously, but that she was secretly casting spells on all of us.

Dr. Thompson's question should be an easy question to answer, right? I mean everyone does something for themselves every now and then, whether it's getting a manicure, taking a nap, or sitting outside on a nice day and reading a book. It shouldn't be that hard for me to think of something, ANYTHING, that I've done for myself recently. Unfortunately, I'm coming up blank.

"Addison?"

Dr. Thompson sits with her hands folded in her lap, waiting for me to answer her. But I can't. I don't have an answer. I haven't done anything for myself in longer than I can remember. I run the bakery every day and sure, it pays the bills and keeps a roof over my head, but I do it for my mom, not for me. I do it because it's what she would have wanted. I go to support meetings every week, and supposedly they're to help me, but they aren't really for me. They're for my dad and because of my dad, and it makes HIM happy that I go to these meetings week after week.

"I want you to do one thing this week. One thing that is just for YOU. One thing that doesn't benefit anyone else but yourself. One thing that doesn't make anyone else happy but you. Do you think you can do that?"

Sitting on the bench in front of the bakery, I stare down at the top sheet of the yellow legal pad that's been sitting in my lap for five minutes. As much as Dr. Thompson's advice usually annoys me, I decided to try out one of her suggestions this week. I just put a batch of banana nut muffins in the oven, and I have twenty-five minutes to myself before I need to go in, take them out, and pack them up for an order. Twenty-five minutes all to myself; one thousand five hundred seconds of uninterrupted time that I can spend on Addison. I knew as soon as Dr. Thompson suggested it what I'd choose to do if I had the time. I would write. I would write until my fingers were sore from holding the pen, and I would write until I had no more words left in me. I would write enough material to fill a hundred yellow legal pads and still have thoughts left for a few more. But here I sit, on a bench in the spring sunshine, unable to write one word. The only thoughts that fill my mind are ones about the bakery and all of my responsibilities—the type of thoughts that remind me I shouldn't be sitting here doing nothing when I have so much other work to do. Obviously I'm not grasping the purpose of this exercise: to do something that makes me happy and that will help pull me out of the black hole I've been in for far too long.

I close my eyes and try to think of something cheerful that has nothing to do with the building behind me, but it's impossible. I put a wall up between my heart and my mind a long time ago and nothing can break through it. I try to feel something other than numb, but I can't do it. If I let just one little feeling in, the rest will follow and my wall will come crashing down, and then I'll feel everything. I can't afford to feel everything. I can't afford to have the weight of all of those emotions crushing me. I have a business to run and bills to pay. At nineteen years old, when all of my former friends are enjoying college and having fun, I have responsibilities that can't be put on the back burner because if I take time for myself, everything will collapse around me.

Frustrated with myself and my failure at "me" time, I open my eyes and see a napkin resting on top of the legal pad in my lap with familiar handwriting on it. The handwriting doesn't affect me as much as the picture drawn underneath the words does. There's a stick figure with its arms open wide and the words "I like it when you smile thiiiiiiiiiiis much" underneath it.

After just a few weeks, I'm used to seeing his familiar scribble on napkins, and I almost expect it and anticipate it so it isn't much of a shock anymore. When he gets up from his corner table and walks out the front door with a wave, I hold my breath and scream at the butterflies in my stomach to pipe down as I head over to the table to clear it and grab the note I know will be waiting for me. What I don't expect to see in my lap is something so reminiscent of my mother that it takes my breath away.

"Mom, I'm seventeen years old. You don't have to pack my lunch for school," I tell her with a roll of my eyes as she pulls a napkin out of the holder on the table and grabs a pen from the junk drawer.

"Nonsense. If I don't pack your lunch, you won't eat. You're skinny enough as it is. Plus, if I didn't pack it, I wouldn't be able to leave you notes," she says with a smile as she draws her usual stick figure on the napkin with its arms open wide and the words "I love you thiiiiiiiiiiis much" written underneath.

"There. Perfect." She folds the napkin in half and sticks it in the brown paper bag. "Now you can go off into the big bad world of high school and tell all of your friends that your mother still writes you love notes and puts them in your lunch."

I shake my head at her, and with a sigh, grab the bag out of her hands and walk toward the door.

"It's a good thing my friends know you, otherwise this would be really embarrassing," I shout to her over my shoulder as I head out to the driveway.

I used to always pretend like it embarrassed me when she did things like that, but honestly, it never did. It made me smile and it made me feel loved. For as long as I could remember, she left those notes in my lunch, around the house, or in my car. For Valentine's Day every year she would buy me a stuffed animal that either held a heart in its arms with the words "I love you thiiiiiiiiis much" on it, or it would speak those words out loud when you pulled its arms apart.

My heart beats erratically in my chest and the words on the napkin in my lap grow blurry as I feel my eyes fill with tears. I will NOT cry. I refuse to cry. If I start, I'll never stop. If I think about her, I'll never stop. It will be a never-ending influx of memories and conversations that will just NEVER STOP.

"Stop, stop, stop, please stop," I whisper to myself over and over as I squeeze my eyes closed and mentally calculate how many dozen cupcakes I need to make to fill next week's order for the Father Daughter dance at the elementary school and how many pounds of sugar, flour, and butter I need to remember to order when the delivery company shows up this week.

I should never have thought about that memory. As soon as I saw those words and the stick figure, I should have crumpled up the napkin and thrown it into the street before my mind opened itself up. I've taught myself to shut everything off in the last year and a half. No memories, no emotions, just keep moving forward and pretend like she never existed. If I pretend like she never existed, I can breathe. If I pretend like she was never real, I can wake up each morning and not feel like my heart is being ripped out of my chest.

"Hey, are you okay? Addison, open your eyes."

I hear his voice right next to me, but I can't open my eyes to look at him. I'm afraid to open them. If I open them, it will all be real. I'll feel the heat of the sun on my skin and the brush of the wind across my face, and I'll know I'm not sleeping. I'll know that I'm awake and alone. I'll know that I haven't been dreaming all this time; that she's really gone and never coming back.

"Addison, come on, open your eyes. Whatever it is, it's okay. It's okay."

I feel his arms around my shoulders, pulling my body up against his on the bench, and I want to relax into him and take the comfort he is offering, but I can't let go of the stiffness in my body. I'm not used to leaning on someone, figuratively OR literally. I smell his cologne and it reminds me of our interaction in the elevator. It reminds me of just how adept he is at making me forget about my problems, and I instantly feel like I can breathe again. I can breathe as long as I can breathe *him* in. I can function because he makes me forget. I just want to forget. I slowly open my eyes, and I'm staring straight into his pale blue ones focusing on me with such concern and worry.

"How did you know I was out here?" I whisper.

He chuckles and then lets out a deep sigh, tightening his arm around my shoulder.

"I went inside for my coffee, and when I didn't see you there, I asked the girl at the counter. Meg, I think she said her name was? Is she a tad bit crazy? I thought she was going to climb over the counter and jump on my back or something when I asked where you were. I saw you sitting out here with your eyes closed so I snuck the napkin on your lap."

His face falls as I suddenly shrug out from under his arm and move a few inches away from him on the bench. Not because I want to, but because I have to. I don't understand why a stranger would want to do something like this for me, and my distrust of people makes me question his motives, but at the same time, his confidence and the familiarity with which he interacts with me makes me want to let my guard down. My brain and my heart are at war with one another, and I can already tell it's going to be a vicious battle. One look into his eyes, and I want to unburden myself of everything. No one has looked at me like that in a long time—like they're concerned for me and just want to make things easier on me. No one wants to help me or cares if I'm okay. They just assume I'm strong and independent because I don't wear my emotions on my sleeve, but they have no idea. Zander barely knows me and he instantly knows I need comfort, even if he doesn't know why. I want to tell him to run as fast as he can because I'm broken. Funny thing though, I don't want him to go. I don't want to do anything that will make him leave because I don't want to be strong anymore. I'm so tired of being strong.

Zander reaches over and pulls the napkin off of my lap, just as quickly as I forgot it was there. That one little piece of paper that had the power to do so much damage and I forgot all about it because he was so focused on me and how he could help me instead of the other way around like everyone else in my life.

I look away from his eyes and focus on his hands while he begins ripping the napkin to shreds in his own lap.

"Why are you doing that?" I ask him softly, watching the stick figure get beheaded and then lose all of his limbs as the torn pieces land in piles on top of his thighs.

"I'm sorry. I shouldn't have done this," he tells me quietly.

I start to feel uncomfortable that he somehow knows why it upset me. He knows that I'm messed up and almost had a panic attack over a stupid napkin drawing. He knows that I have entirely too many issues, and he should just get up and walk away right now.

"Obviously I need to work on my artistic skills. This stick figure was atrocious. If someone handed that to me I would have gotten upset too. His head was too big and he had googly eyes."

He says it so seriously that it strikes me as the funniest thing I've ever heard, and I want to laugh out loud, but that feeling is foreign to me. I haven't laughed out loud in a long time. I bite my lip to hold back my smile as he scoops up the pile of ripped apart napkin and crumples the pieces in his fist, holding it up in the air.

"As God is my witness, I shall never draw stick figures again!" he shouts loudly.

The fierce look on his face and the handful of strangers walking by, who jump and take off walking in the opposite direction as fast as they can, push me over the edge. The laughter bubbles out of my throat before I can stop it. The sound is so strange to me that I immediately clamp my hand over my mouth to contain it, but it's no use.

"Don't run from your fears! Bad stick figure drawing is serious, people!" he yells.

"Oh my God, stop!" I laugh at him.

He lowers his hand and studies my face with a smile, cocking his head to the side.

"Only if you promise to never hold that laugh in again," he tells me softly.

I swallow roughly at the sweetness of his words, trying to ignore the pull I feel toward him by attempting to keep things light and not so intense.

"Are you going to say something cheesy again like 'you're beautiful when you laugh?'" I ask him with a smile, unable to believe that this guy can make me go from completely panicked one minute to laughing hysterically the next. The power he has over me should scare me, but for some reason it doesn't. He reminds me what it's like to forget about my problems and just laugh like no one is watching. He makes me feel alive again.

"I might. I've been known to throw out a little cheese now and again."

I shake my head at him and glance down at my watch, realizing I have thirty seconds to get inside and remove the muffins from the oven.

"I have to go. Thanks for…well, just…thanks," I tell him sheepishly as I get up from the bench and hurry to the door of the bakery before I make a fool of myself.

"YOU'RE STUNNING WHEN YOU SMILE AND LAUGH, ADDISON!" he yells to me. I let out an embarrassed laugh as I open the door and walk inside. I catch my reflection in the mirror right inside the store, but all I see is an average girl. I'm 5'4 with boring, brown, wavy hair that hangs past my shoulders, unless it's in my usual messy ponytail. I have a dusting of freckles on my nose and my mother's gray eyes, which I've always thought were my only redeeming quality. But Zander thinks I'm stunning. He sees something that I've never seen.

I may not have figured out how to shut off my mind to take some time for myself and do some writing, but right now, it doesn't seem to bother me very much.

Chapter Five
Possibility

"I can't tell you whether or not what your feeling is right or wrong, Addison. I can only give you the tools you need to make that decision for yourself."

Dr. Thompson's cryptic response to my question about the strange connection I feel towards Zander so soon doesn't help me in the least. I want her to tell me that it's crazy how comfortable I feel with him and it's pointless to waste time I don't even have thinking about him.

"Do you feel like he's someone you could eventually trust and confide in?" she asks.

"I have no idea. I don't even know anything about him."

Dr. Thompson laughs lightly at my frustrated response.

"Then ask him. Get to know him. Open yourself up to someone. Maybe the reason why you feel so comfortable with him so soon is because you know he doesn't know anything about you. You don't have to be worried about the fact that he *might* judge you or he *might* pity you," she explains.

"You make it sound like he wouldn't do those things if he knew everything about me."

Dr. Thompson shrugs. "I don't know if he would or wouldn't, but neither do you. And you never will if you don't give him a chance. He could very well prove you wrong."

She makes it sound so easy. She doesn't understand that both of those ideas scare me more than I care to admit. What if he turns out to be someone I could trust? What then? I would only end up hurting him when he realizes the type of person I've become.

"Dude, are you feeling okay? I haven't seen you smile this much since...um, ever. Did your doctor change your meds or something?" Meg asks curiously as I wipe the smile from my face, not even realizing that I'm doing it. I can't help it. It's been two weeks since I sat outside in the sun with Zander and laughed harder than I had in a long time.

No matter how hard I tried not to think about it, I was excited to get up this morning and come to the bakery, knowing I would get to see him. He's been in every single day for the past two weeks, and instead of just sitting at his usual table, he stood next to the counter and watched me work each time.

"So, what are you making now?" Zander asked as he drained his coffee cup and pitched it behind the counter into the trashcan.

"White chocolate macadamia nut cookies," I told him as I crossed it off my list. The peanut butter chocolate chunk cookies I'd just finished with were now cooling on the counter next to him.

I turned around to face him and caught him shoveling two cookies into his mouth.

"Hey! Hands off the merchandise," I scolded as I smacked his hand when he reached for another one.

"But you put them right in front of me!"

He crossed his arms in front of his chest and pouted. His mouth turned down in a frown. It was impossible not to laugh at how dramatic he was acting.

I moved the tray out of his reach. "I put them in front of you to cool, not so you could inhale them."

"Just think of me as quality control. You wouldn't want to feed your customers bad cookies, would you? Obviously someone needs to make sure all of the cookies are delicious. It's okay, you don't have to pay me. The obvious joy on your face is thanks enough."

He's left a napkin behind every single day when I'm not looking, and I still pretend like they annoy me so Meg will get off my case. It's hard to be irritated, though, when yesterday's napkin said he loved my dimples when I smile.

I've started tacking each and every napkin to the bulletin board in my room, but I'll never tell anyone that. I'll never admit that each night after I type my note to my mom before I go to sleep, I stare at all of the napkins and the messages written on them. I read through each and every one of them before I crawl into bed, and for some strange reason, it's helped keep the bad dreams away. Ever since I received the first napkin from Zander, I've stopped having the same recurring dream that my mother is still alive and wants nothing to do with me. I no longer wake up each night with tears on my cheeks and a scream in my throat as I try to shake off the remnants of the dream where I'm chasing after her, calling her name, but she won't turn around or acknowledge me. I've spent plenty of time on the internet researching what this dream could mean, and all of the answers leave me with a feeling of dread. All of the emotions I've kept buried for so long are manifesting themselves into the one thing I'm most afraid of: that my mother is ashamed of my behavior and that's why she doesn't acknowledge me in my dreams.

I ignore Meg's incessant chatter behind me about a rude customer that was in the store the day before. I look at the clock and wonder if Zander will be on time today or running late again like yesterday. I don't even know what he does for a living. Or how old he is. Or his last name. Jesus, this is crazy and I probably DO need to change my meds. We've been talking for weeks and haven't spoken about anything of importance.

The bell above the door dings, and I can't keep the smile off of my face even with Meg standing right by my side and staring at me with her mouth wide open because I'm practically bouncing up and down with happiness when I see him. Zander returns my smile and walks up to the counter.

"So, my mom's birthday is coming up and I really want to bake her a cake," he says in greeting as I pour his usual cup of coffee, and he takes a seat at the one and only barstool on the other side of the counter that Meg brought out last week from the storage room just for him.

"Um, yay?" I reply in confusion, not really sure why he's telling me this.

"Here's the thing. I can make a mean piece of cinnamon and sugar toast and my microwave chicken nuggets are TO DIE FOR, but other than that, I'm kind of clueless in the kitchen," he says with a sheepish smile.

He looks down at his coffee and busies himself stirring in his sugar. I can see a faint blush on his cheeks, and it suddenly occurs to me that he's embarrassed. I don't know why, but it's the cutest thing I've ever seen. He always seems so confident and sure of himself, and it's a little intimidating. But right now he's on my turf, and he's asking for my help with something I'm pretty damn good at.

"Do you want me to bake something for her?"

He looks up at me, and I can't help starring as he tugs his bottom lip into his mouth.

"That would be cheating. And she would totally know I cheated, and I'd never hear the end of it. She still likes to tell everyone the story about when I was in kindergarten and tried to bribe my bus driver with chocolate chip cookies if she would do my homework for me for a week. Store bought chocolate chip cookies, mind you. Imagine what she would do with the knowledge that I had a professional baker make her a cake and tried to pass it off as my own?" he asks me in horror.

He rests his hands flat on the counter and leans across it so he's closer to me. I hold my breath as he stares deeply into my eyes.

"Teach me how to bake. Help me, Addison. You're my only hope," he whispers seriously.

I swallow thickly and feel my heart speed up in my chest as he looks at me imploringly. I don't even know what he just said to me; all I can think about is listening to his soothing voice, even if he's just reciting the alphabet or reading the phone book.

Meg suddenly laughs loudly, and I jump in surprise, not even realizing she's still standing there next to me, watching this whole exchange. I take a step away from the counter and mentally shake myself out of the trance Zander has put me in with his pretty face and his pretty voice.

Stupid pretty boy.

"Oh my God, you totally just quoted Star Wars! You, my friend, go straight to the top of the awesome list," Meg tells him with a big smile as she moves next to me and wraps her left arm around my shoulder and clamps her right hand tightly over my mouth. "Addison would love to teach you how to bake. The shop closes at six-thirty tonight, so be here by six-forty-five. Just knock on the back door."

I struggle against Meg's arm and try to talk around her hand against my mouth, but she's not having any of it. She tightens her hold and brings the heel of her boot down on top of my toe. I let out a squeak of pain from behind her hand and shoot her a dirty look with my eyes.

Zander looks back and forth between us and laughs.

"Well, that's very nice of Addison to offer her services. Meg, could you tell her that I greatly appreciate it and I will be here at six-forty-five on the dot?"

He winks and smiles at me before bringing the cup of coffee up to his mouth and taking a sip. I forget about struggling and I sag against Meg as we both watch him get off of the stool, turn, and walk out of the shop.

"That guy has a great ass," Meg says softly with a sigh, her hand still over my mouth having forgotten to remove it because she's too busy staring at all that pretty. I just nod my head silently in agreement to her ass statement. We both stand there in a daze, staring at the door he just walked through until the timer goes off on one of the ovens and the reality of what Meg just did hits me like a two-by-four to the face. I bang my hip into hers and elbow her in the side until she drops her arms from around me with an irritated shout of pain.

"Hey, what was that for?" she complains as she rubs her side.

"Are you kidding me? ARE YOU FREAKING KIDDING ME?" I whisper yell at her so the customers won't hear my outburst. "Why would you do that? Oh my God, oh my God, oh my God!"

Meg rolls her eyes at me as I start pacing back and forth behind the counter, wondering how quickly I can get a passport and leave the country.

"Seriously, chill out. He's just a guy. A very cute guy who obviously likes you. All morning you've been walking around here in a creeptastic cloud of happiness and it's because of HIM."

She walks over and stands directly in front of me so I have to stop my manic pacing and stare at her.

"You and I both know that life sucks. At any minute something crappy could happen, and the two of us just sit around just waiting for the crappy and expecting it. When something good happens, we have to reach out and grab it, otherwise our lives will turn into one giant run-on sentence of daily sucks. I'm tired of the sucks, Addy. Come on, be tired of the sucks with me."

She wags her eyebrows at me, and I let out a sigh.

"Come on, all your friends are doing it," she says with a laugh as she reaches out and shoves my shoulder.

I chuckle at her exuberance as she skips around me and heads back into the kitchen to remove the cupcakes—that are probably burnt now—from the oven.

She's right. I know she's right. Life is a daily crapshoot and you never know what's going to happen next. I used to love the thrill of never knowing what life would bring and the excitement of waking up to a brand new day and all of the possibilities. Now I spend each day full of dread that something bad will happen. I wake up each morning wondering what will go wrong next. I don't enjoy the little things anymore because I know something bigger will come along that will swallow up those little things and make them disappear like they were never there. What's the point in enjoying those little things when they'll be gone soon?

I don't know if Zander is a little thing or a big thing: a possibility or a liability. I've made sure to keep the guessing game out of life by shutting off my emotions and just doing what I need to do to make it through each day. I'm suddenly very aware of how empty my life has been lately. The idea of spending an evening alone with him where he might ask me questions I won't know how to answer scares the hell out of me. But at the same time, I feel a bubble of nerves and butterflies in my stomach that have nothing to do with fear and everything to do with the thrill of the unknown and where it might lead. Maybe there's hope for me yet.

Chapter Six

Hurt

"Would you say that you go through each day expecting that the people around you are going to let you down?" Dr. Thompson asks me before she takes a sip of her Panera coffee.

I shrug as I pick a hangnail. "Sure. It's easier that way and it just makes sense."

I glance up when she doesn't say anything and am glad I don't see a look of pity on her face. The only reason I continue coming to Dr. Thompson each week is because she never pities me. She's concerned for me about the things I've been through, but she never feels sorry for me. I can't stand anyone feeling sorry for me, like I'm this sad, pathetic little girl that people need to coddle.

"Tell me how that makes sense, Addison? I want to understand what goes on in that pretty head of yours when you think about these things. And stop picking at your nails," she scolds as she sets her cup down on the table next to her chair.

I immediately pull my hands apart and smack them down on either side of me on the couch with a guilty look on my face, just like I used to do when my mom would reprimand me for the exact same thing. I huff irritably and cross my arms in front of me.

"Look, if I go into things expecting people to suck, when they finally DO suck, it's not that bad. They acted just like I thought they would, I'm not surprised, and I can just move on. If I walked around every day with my head in the clouds, thinking everyone in my life will never let me down and will never hurt me, it won't be long before they show their true colors and disappoint me. It's easier to just accept the fact that I'm the only one looking out for me."

I finish with my explanation and wait for her to tell me how wrong I am—about life, about the people around me, about my opinions. Just like every week, though, she never does what I expect her to do.

"I would have done the exact same thing if I were you. It's tough being so young and having the people close to you let you down so many times when you need them most. Just try and do me a favor. Keep an open mind. Sometimes, people will surprise you."

I feel like I'm going to throw up from nerves. I've looked at the clock a hundred times since I put the "closed" sign on the front door. Before I can change my mind and run out of the building, there's a knock on the back door. Looking quickly around the kitchen to make sure it's not too much of a disaster, I take a few deep breaths and walk to the door and turn the deadbolt.

"I brought you flowers," Zander says with a smile as I open the door. I laugh and feel instantly at ease when he pulls two bags of flour out from behind his back and hands them to me.

"Wow, how very romantic of you," I tell him.

I cringe and want to take the word back immediately. Why did I say romantic? This isn't a date. Nothing about this is romantic. He didn't ask me out; he asked if I could help him. Big difference. I'm teaching him how to bake. The end. He doesn't even acknowledge my word choice or notice the turmoil going on in my brain over one simple word. He just hands over the bags of flour and walks through the door and farther into the kitchen.

I close the back door and turn to set the bags on the wood block island in the middle of the kitchen, ignoring his stare as he watches me move about. I know if I look at him right now I'm going to feel like an idiot. Walking over to my iPod dock on the side counter, I turn on Pandora, switching it from the angry chick rock station to just plain rock. Something tells me Zander wouldn't appreciate listening to a bunch of women screaming about hating life and how all men suck.

"Bringing you flour is the least I could do. You're saving my ass by doing this."

He comes over and stands next to me as I begin setting out mixing bowls, measuring cups, and all the ingredients we'll need to make a cake.

"Where's the box of cake mix?" he asks in confusion as he picks up a canister of baking powder and looks it over.

"Cake mix? You can't say something like that here. That's blasphemy. Why did you bring me flour if you thought we were using a cake mix?" I ask him with a laugh as he continues to stand there staring at me in fear while I organize the ingredients on the counter.

"You work in a bakery and I figured you could always use flour for other things. I was trying to be cute and think outside the box. But not outside the cake mix box. Is it too late to buy my mom some jewelry or a gift certificate to a spa?" he asks in a panic.

"Oh hush. You'll be fine. We're making the cake from scratch because that's the best way to do it."

I separate all of the items on the counter so we each have one of the same.

"Did you forget about the part where I can't cook? This is not going to end well," he says nervously as I hand him two eggs and point to his mixing bowl.

"Did *you* forget the part where I run a bakery? This is going to end awesome. Less talking, more paying attention," I tell him as I indicate with my hands that he should follow what I'm doing as I crack the eggs and measure the sugar, flour, butter, baking powder, vanilla, and milk. I hand him a wooden spoon and we both silently stir our mixtures. I thought I would feel more uncomfortable alone with Zander than I actually do. Aside from my stupid "romantic" slip, being here with him makes me feel anything but nervous. Standing next to him, listening to the music playing softly, our arms brushing up against each other every so often as we mix and stir, I feel at ease. He has a calming effect on me that seems familiar. I hadn't really noticed it before, but every time he speaks, something tickles the back of my mind. Like a memory trying to surface through the fog, but I just can't make it appear. I ignore the nagging sensation and just let myself be in the moment for once, not worrying about anything else around me. We talk about nonsensical things like our favorite celebrities, favorite movies, best book we ever read, and the places we'd like to travel to someday. In between our talking, I give him instructions and tips on baking. It feels so natural being here with him like this, talking easily and trying my hand at flirting.

Unfortunately, the universe has a funny way of knowing when I'm starting to let my guard down. As soon as I open my mouth to ask Zander about his job, my iPod starts playing a haunting melody—one I'm all too familiar with.

"This is a great song. Have you heard the version by Johnny Cash?" Zander asks.

I'm too busy being sucked into a memory to answer him. A memory that causes me to drop my bowl of batter and clutch both of my hands to my chest to stop the ache in my heart, to stop the remembrance of a day that I've tried to never think of again. It's impossible to use my switch now and turn everything off. With Zander here, my switch is broken.

I turned the volume up as high as it would go in my Honda Civic as I drove my best friend Casey and I to school after spending the previous night at her house. It was the last day before Christmas break which was why my mom agreed to let me spend the night on a school night.

"Oh my gosh, I hate this song. It's so depressing," Casey yelled over the music.

"You're insane! This is Hurt by Nine Inch Nails and it's awesome!" I argued with her before I began to sing along.

Halfway into the chorus, during a quieter part of the song, I heard my cell phone ring in the center console. I stopped at a stop sign and grabbed it, noticing that I had three missed calls from my dad.

"Hey, Dad, what's up?" I answered as I quickly turned down the volume on the radio.

"SHE'S GONE! OH MY GOD, SHE'S GONE!" my dad yelled into the phone.

I'd never heard my dad like that before, and my stomach immediately dropped when I heard the sobs in his voice as he continued to cry and yell.

"Dad, what are you talking about? What's going on?"

Casey leaned toward me and gave me a questioning look, but I just shook my head at her. I had no idea what was happening and I was scared to death.

"Your mom, oh God, I think your mom's gone. Oh my God. Oh God help me," my dad cried.

"WHAT? Dad, what are you talking about?"

My hands shook and I felt Casey reach over and wrap her arm around my shoulder.

"I can't wake her up, Addison. I think she's gone. Oh, Jesus. Oh my God."

My breath whooshed out of me, and I clenched my jaw as hard as I could so I wouldn't break down on the phone with him. He was hysterical and I couldn't process what he was saying to me.

"I'm coming home. I'm coming home right now. Okay, Dad? I'll be home as soon as I can," I reassured him.

He continued to cry and mumble incoherently about her being gone before I heard the dial tone in my ear. I pulled the phone away and stare at it.

This couldn't be happening. It wasn't real. I just saw her last night and she was fine. She was healthy and perfect and we talked about baking Christmas cookies. She just got a clean bill of health from her oncologist last week. We just celebrated the second anniversary of her being in remission. This wasn't real, it wasn't real, it wasn't real.

"Addison, what happened?"

Casey's voice made me jump. I forgot she was in the car with me. I slowly turned and faced her, not wanting to say the words out loud, not wanting to believe that this was happening.

"I think my mom's gone. I...I think she's dead."

Casey gasped and I watched in a daze as the tears started to fall from her eyes. I couldn't cry. I couldn't believe it was real. It wasn't real.

"It's not real. It's not real. It's not real," I whispered over and over to myself.

My cell phone rang again, and I immediately answered it. I hoped with everything in me that this was just some cruel joke that someone decided to play on me.

"Addison, it's Aunt Katie," my aunt said softly. I could hear the tears and sadness in her voice but I ignored it.

"What's going on? Did you talk to Dad? This isn't happening, right?"

My aunt let out a small sob and I squeezed my eyes closed.

"You need to come home, sweetie."

I handed the phone over to Casey without even answering her. I heard Casey talking softly with my aunt, but I ignored it. The song was *still playing on the radio and all I heard were the words that Casey just said were so depressing only moments ago.*

Everyone I love goes away, in the end.

I leaned forward and rested my head on the steering wheel and screamed as loud and as long as I could. I screamed until I had no voice left. I screamed until I couldn't hear anything but the sound of my screams echoing through my head.

"Addison, hey, it's okay. Shhhh, you're okay. I'm right here, Addison."

Zander's soothing voice by my ear brings me back from the past, but there's something about those words. Something about the way he says them that gives me goose bumps. He's said those exact words to me before. I know he has. But that's not possible. I can remember every single conversation we've ever had, every word he's ever spoken to me. What is happening to me? What is wrong with me?

"I think I'm going crazy," I whisper to him when I finally find my voice. My throat hurts, and I'm immediately embarrassed. I know that feeling. I must have been screaming.

"It's okay, we're all a little bit crazy," he reassures me softly before pulling me closer and placing a kiss on top of my head.

I suddenly notice that we're sitting on the floor of the kitchen in a puddle of cake batter. It's all over my jeans, and since Zander is right next to me, it's now all over his as well as his shoes. I'm mortified that this happened. It's been so long since I had an episode like this and now, ever since meeting Zander, it's happened twice.

"I'm sorry. Oh my gosh, I'm so sorry. I'm such an idiot," I ramble in shame, tears prickling my eyes as I pull out of his arms and attempt to get up off of the floor so I can run and hide in a closet somewhere and never have to face him again.

Unfortunately, my feet slide right through the slippery batter that coats the floor and I flop back down on my butt, causing batter to splatter on the front of Zander's T-shirt.

I stare at his shirt in horror and watch as he slowly looks down at the front of him. Reaching over, I try to wipe the mess off of his shirt but forget all about the fact that my hands smacked down in batter when I fell. Instead of helping him, I just get him messier by smearing more goo onto him.

"Oh no," I whisper in dismay. I can feel my chin start to quiver, and I know if I don't leave right now, I'm going to start crying. I will NOT cry in front of him.

This night just went from bad to the worst night in history. He's going to get up and run out of here so fast that all I'll see is a cloud of dust in his wake. It would be easier for me if I never had to see him again and relive this horrifying nightmare of having a break down in front of him and then spilling cake batter all over his clothes, but just that thought alone depresses me.

"You are in such big trouble now," Zander finally says quietly as he looks up at me. I bite my lip, waiting for him to tell me what a freak I am, but instead his mouth curls in a menacing grin. Before I can apologize to him again, a handful of batter is mashed against the side of my face from Zander's hand.

I gasp in shock as the cold liquid drips down the side of my face and drops down the front of my V-neck T-shirt.

Zander chuckles at the look of complete shock on my face, and without thinking about my actions, I quickly scoop up some of the batter by my hip and mirror his actions, smacking the mixture on one of his cheeks with a maniacal laugh. This situation is just too crazy for me to even comprehend right now.

We sit there quietly staring at one another with wide eyes until suddenly we both burst out laughing, each of us scrambling to wipe up more spilled batter from the floor and throw it at one another. I start screaming and laughing when a pile of it lands on top of my head, and Zander lets out a yelp when I reach over and smear a handful through his hair.

"Oh my gosh, UNCLE! UNCLE! I have cake batter in my eye!" Zander complains with a laugh as he holds up his messy hands in front of him in a sign of surrender.

"Shut it! I have cake batter in my ear," I reply with a giggle.

He wipes one of his hands off on his jeans and reaches over, using the heel of his hand to get some of the mess off of my cheek. His hand is warm and soft as it sweeps against my skin, and I instantly feel cherished as he touches me. I've been craving attention like this from someone for so long that even the simple act of cleaning off my face fills me with unexpected appreciation for him and the care he takes with me. When he finishes getting most of it off, he doesn't move his hand away from me; instead he cups the side of my face and brushes his thumb back and forth over my cheekbone.

I swallow thickly and hold my breath as he stares into my eyes then slowly moves his gaze down to my lips. I quickly wet them with my tongue, and I hear him make a low groaning sound in his throat.

"I really want to kiss you right now," he whispers, still staring at my lips.

My heart beats frantically in my chest. I should tell him no. I should tell him he doesn't want to get messed up with me because it won't end well. I should tell him he's too good to get involved with me. There are so many things I *should* do, but right now I can't do anything but slowly nod my head in response to his words.

"Okay," I reply softly.

He slowly moves his face toward mine, and I close my eyes, the anticipation of feeling his lips on mine too much to take with my eyes open. I can feel his breath on my face and the first tentative touch of his lips. A shiver runs up my spine. His lips are soft and warm as he presses them against mine, and I let out a sigh against his mouth when he wraps his other arm around my waist and slides me across the floor closer to him. All the bad thoughts fly from my mind, and nothing consumes me right now except Zander: Zander's touch, Zander's lips, Zander's hands… He surrounds me and makes all of the bad things disappear. He deepens the kiss with a groan and tightens his hold around my waist. My arms tangle around his neck, and I kiss him back with everything in me. Every feeling, every thought, every emotion—I pour it all into this kiss.

"Addison! What the hell is going on?"

The angry sound of my dad's voice cuts through the haze of pleasure that envelops me, as Zander and I quickly break apart.

I stare at my father in shock as he stands in the doorway of the kitchen, looking down at Zander and me in irritation. He wasn't supposed to be out of rehab for another two weeks, and I feel a wave of fury wash over me when I realize that he most likely skipped out on it again.

Zander's words from earlier in the evening suddenly pop into my mind at that moment. When he said, "This is not going to end well," I wonder if he had any idea just how true that statement would turn out to be.

Chapter Seven
Time and Time Again

"Maybe he really is turning over a new leaf this time, Addison."

I roll my eyes at Dr. Thompson and cross my arms over my chest.

"You don't think people can change?" she asks softly, seeing the irritation on my face.

"Who knows? It's not like I've had much experience lately with people changing for the better. No one does what they say they will, and no one lives up to their promises."

I pick at some imaginary pieces of lint on my shirt while Dr. Thompson writes on her notepad. One of these days I should just get up and grab that thing from her to see if she's actually writing down things about me or playing tic-tac-toe with herself.

"That's true. Not everyone in your life will always do what you expect of them. Sometimes they'll let you down, and sometimes, even though they tell you that they love you, they do things that prove otherwise. You just have to decide whether or not you have enough room left in your heart for them. Enough space to let them in and show them what you need from them. As much as we want them to, our loved ones can't read our minds. If they don't know what we want from them or what we need from them, they are never going to be able to give it to us."

I already know what I want from my father. I want him to man up and make himself accountable for his actions. I want him to be able to go back in time and erase all of the bad decisions he's made and take away the hurtful things he's said to me that caused me to turn into the person I am today.

I know that's not possible though. And frankly, I don't know if I have the strength to move things around in my life to make that extra space for him that I filled with responsibilities since he hit rock bottom.

Zander quickly gets up from the floor and reaches down to grab me under my arm and help me to my feet. My dad stands by the door looking back and forth between us. His head suddenly jerks to Zander's face, and he stares at him for a moment in confusion, squinting his eyes and studying his face for so long that Zander finally looks away uncomfortably.

"Do I know you from somewhere?" my dad asks, breaking the awkward silence in the room.

Zander laughs uneasily and doesn't make eye contact with him while he busies himself trying to brush off some of the cake batter from his hands off onto his pants.

"Eh, people say that all the time. I guess I have a common face." He turns away from my dad to face me and speaks softly so he can't hear us. "I'm gonna get going. I'll call you later."

I look at him questioningly, trying to remember if I ever gave him my number.

"Meg slipped me your cell phone number the last time I was here. Didn't want to make myself seem even more stalkerish by calling you without your knowledge," he says quietly with a sweet smile before he turns and quickly walks past my father with his head down.

"Sir," he mumbles to my dad in good-bye as he rushes by him and out the back door.

I wait until the door clicks shut behind Zander before I finally face my father. I'm angry that he's here, I'm angry that my time with Zander was cut short, especially when I just quite possibly received one of the best kisses of my life, and I'm angry that he made Zander feel uncomfortable. I'm angry and confused and I'm full of cake batter. I don't want him to be here. My life is good without him here. I'm used to him being gone and I'm used to my routine. Having him back is just going to mess everything up.

"What are you doing here?"

I don't even bother to hide the contempt in my voice. I'm done trying to keep what I think of him a secret. It obviously hasn't helped him in the past, so maybe if he knows how much I don't want him or need him here, it will finally get through to him.

"I got out of rehab early. My counselor said I made great progress and she's confident that I have all of the tools I need to be healthy, so here I am," he tells me with a smile.

Like it's that simple. Like some stranger who hasn't lived with him and hasn't dealt with his addiction day in and day out can really make an accurate assessment of him after only a few weeks. Each time he's been in rehab they've given him a new counselor. And each time, those idiots think they've cured him. I'm sure this time isn't any different.

"I've got it this time, Addison, I really do."

I sigh and turn away from him, walking over to the sink to wash my hands. I can't look at him right now. Even though I've learned in the last year not to trust or believe anything that comes out of his mouth, he still knows how to make me wonder. He still knows what to say to make that little voice in the back of my head say, "Maybe he's right. Maybe this time he really does have it."

I'm disappointed in myself for even allowing that voice to have a say anymore. She's been wrong so much that I think it's high time she takes a hike.

"I'm going to be here for you. I'm going to take over the responsibilities here at the shop and everything is going to go back to normal," he tells me earnestly.

Normal? Like he even knows what that is. We haven't been normal since my mom died, and I find it hard to believe we ever will be again.

I dry my hands on a towel and then take it over to start cleaning up the floor. My dad rushes over to my side and takes the towel from my hands.

"Here, I've got this. You go ahead and finish getting cleaned up. I'll take care of things here."

I snatch the towel back out of his hand and squat down to the floor and begin wiping up the mess. "No, *I've* got it. Just like always."

I hear my dad sigh in defeat as he stands above me and watches. I walk back and forth between the mess and the sink, rinsing out the towel each time, until all of the cake batter is finally gone.

"Addison, please. Just let me help you. Give me a chance," he pleads, bringing some of the dirty bowls and measuring cups over to me at the sink.

I whirl around to face him and cross my arms over my chest. My hands are shaking with fury, and if I don't keep them glued to my body, I'll probably do something incredibly stupid like throw the second bowl of cake batter at him.

"I've given you plenty of chances. *Plenty*. And each time you've thrown my trust and my faith in you back in my face like it didn't even matter," I tell him angrily.

"I know, believe me, I know. I'm well aware of the fact that I have a lot to prove to you. And I'll do it, Addison. I swear I will prove to you that you can trust me."

The voice in my head is finally silent. She must have finally gotten sick of the bullshit too.

"I'm going home," I tell him without responding to his empty promises. I turn away from him and walk toward the door, leaving the dirty dishes piled in the sink. Normally, I never leave a mess in the kitchen before I leave at night because I don't want to have to deal with it the next morning. Right now I just want to get out of here and away from my father. The dishes will have to wait.

"Why don't you just ride home with me? We can come back tomorrow morning and you can get your car then," he tells me, trying one last time for us to spend some quality time together.

It occurs to me then that my father has no idea I moved out of my childhood home. He has no idea that I couldn't take one more day in that house because I saw my mother everywhere, and yet she was nowhere to be found. He made certain of that the day after she died. We had come home from making all of the funeral arrangements, and while family and friends stopped by to bring food and other useless items they thought would cure our broken hearts, my father began packing every single item of my mother's away. Clothes, shoes, jewelry, pictures, knickknacks…anything and everything that she ever touched was packed away into totes and immediately taken to Goodwill. Every trace of my mother was given away to strangers, and by the end of that day it was like she never even existed.

After my father went into rehab this last time, I couldn't take being in that house anymore. I couldn't take walking in the door and feeling like I just didn't belong there. Without my mom, I didn't belong anywhere.

"I don't live at the house anymore. I have an apartment over by the mall," I told him as I grabbed my purse from the counter and dug my keys out of the bottom.

"What? What do you mean you don't live at home anymore?" my dad asks in confusion.

I finally find my keys, turn the knob, and open the door.

"I mean, I don't live at home anymore," I tell him with spite. I should just walk out and end it on that note, but I can't. I've always been the type of person who needs to make sure my point is hammered home, always making sure I have the last word. At least one thing has remained constant with my personality. I turn around and face him one last time before I go. "You erased every trace of her from that house. Why the hell *would* I want to continue living there?"

I don't even need to say her name; he visibly winces like he's in pain when I mention her.

"I'll lock everything up," he tells me, turning away and walking over to the wall where the light switch is. He shuts off all of the lights except for the security light over the back door where I'm still standing. "I want you to take the day off tomorrow. I'll take care of things here."

Just like every other time I've brought her up, he completely changes the subject. He doesn't want to talk about her; he doesn't want to acknowledge her. And he wonders why I am the way I am. He wonders why I'm such a different person, why I'm so closed off now, and why I shut down.

I take my cues from him. I've learned how to close myself off so I don't have to deal with the pain.

"No, I'm working tomorrow. You have no idea what needs to be done."

He raises his eyebrow at me and attempts to be humorous. "Sweetie, I own the shop, and I worked here for enough years to know how things are supposed to go. I'm pretty sure your old man can handle it while you go have fun and be a teenager."

He smiles at me, but I don't return his joviality. He doesn't have any clue that I don't remember how to be a teenager or have fun. It's like he doesn't even remember all of the responsibilities he stuck me with in the last year.

"I'm going to be around a whole lot more, Addison. I'm going to prove to you that I can do this," he promises me softly as I turn away from him and walk through the door.

"I'll believe it when I see it," I mumble loud enough for him to hear before the door slams shut behind me.

After I peel the sticky clothes off of me and take a long, hot shower, I sit down at my computer and power it up, logging in to Facebook and going right to her page to type my usual nighttime private message to her.

Dear Mom:

I wish you were here. You're the only one who understands. The only one I can talk to about anything. I miss you, every single day, every single second.

Love,

Addison

After the message is sent, I power off my computer and curl up in bed on my side, staring at the napkin notes on my bulletin board. I think about the things my dad said to me and wonder how long it will be before I'm sniffing his water bottles, checking for vodka, and looking through his wallet for receipts to the liquor store. I wonder how much more I have left in me. I wonder when it happens this time, because I'm sure it will, if I'll be strong enough to just write him out of my life for good, shut him out and never give him a second thought. My eyes lids start to get heavy, and before I can close them for the night, my cell phone vibrates on the table next to my bed.

The number isn't one I recognize or have programmed in my phone, and my heart beats rapidly in my chest knowing it's Zander and is thrilled that he actually kept his promise of a phone call. At the same time, though, I'm nervous to talk to him again after tonight. I broke down, he kissed me, and then my dad showed up and made everything awkward. I don't know if I'm ready to talk to him about my dad yet. I don't know if I'm ready to let him into that part of my life that I've kept hidden for so long.

I quickly reach over and answer the phone, bringing it close to my ear as I snuggle further under the covers.

"I didn't wake you, did I?"

Zander's soft voice brings a smile to my face, and my melancholy thoughts from moments ago are immediately forgotten.

"Nope, but I am in bed," I tell him with a smile.

He's quiet on the other end for so long that I pull the phone away, wondering if the call was dropped.

"Zander? Are you still there?" I ask when I see the call is still connected.

"Sorry. I lost all train of thought when you told me you were in bed."

I laugh at his words and feel my face heating up with a blush, thankful that I'm on the phone with him and not standing right in front of him so he can't see what his words do to me.

"I swear I won't ask you what you're wearing. Maybe. I think. Okay, I'll give it the old college try, but I'm sorry, I can't make any promises," he tells me with a laugh.

I bite my lip, and even though I have no idea what I'm doing, I quickly decide to have a little fun with him. I've never had time for a relationship and even if I did, I've always purposely avoided them. I've never had any guy in my life like this who made me feel comfortable enough to flirt with or try my hand at teasing. Covering my hand over my eyes to try and force my embarrassment level down a few notches, I give it a shot.

"How about I make it easy on you so you don't go back on your promise? I'm wearing a pair of pink boy shorts and a matching pink tank top, and I'm under the covers. Oh, and I'm not wearing a bra," I tell him boldly, my eyes still squeezing closed as I cringe at my brashness.

"Oh my God," he whispers into the phone. "You're going to be the death of me, Sugar."

My eyes pop open when he calls me Sugar. My mom is the only one who ever used a nickname with me, and she always called me Sweets.

~ᗞ~

"Have a good day at school, Sweets!"

"Hey, Sweets, you want to help me make some chocolate chip cookies?"

～⌒

Hearing Zander call me by a nickname synonymous with the one my mom always used for me makes me feel special and unique—something I haven't felt in so long that I almost forgot what it feels like. I realize quickly that I like the sound of it on Zander's lips. But that's not really a surprise since I like anything that has to do with his lips, especially after that kiss in the bakery. Despite the confrontation with my father, that kiss is all I've been able to think about.

"So, I need to ask you something, and I have a feeling it's going to either make you hang up on me or think I'm crazy," he finally says.

My guard immediately locks back into place when he says this. I'm nervous he's going to ask me something about my dad, ask who he was, or why I didn't introduce him, or why in all the months he's come into the bakery (before we ever even spoke) has he never seen my father here. But just like always, Zander surprises me.

"So, we're having a little get-together for my mom's birthday this weekend at my parent's house. And since you were so awesome at teaching me how to throw cake batter all over the kitchen, I feel it's only right that you come with me so I can show off my mad cake batter flinging skills," he explains.

He really *is* crazy. I'm still in shock that he didn't run away during my freak out and can hardly believe he wanted to kiss me AND he called when he said he would. And now he wants me to meet his parents?

"I don't know if that's such a good idea," I reply nervously.

"Sorry, not only is it a good idea, it's a genius idea. If I bake this cake and it ends up tasting like old gym shoes, you'll be there to save the day."

Okay, now it makes sense. He doesn't want his mother's birthday to be cake-less. If he takes his own personal baker with him, he can make sure that doesn't happen. Maybe that kiss didn't mean as much to him as it did to me. I don't like the feelings of insecurity floating around in my brain as I sit here second-guessing what this thing is between us. I'm not used to feeling so girly and needy.

"Plus, I really want you to be there. I want to spend more time with you, and I want you to meet my family," he tells me softly after I'd already convinced myself he was only asking to make sure his mom had cake.

I don't say anything right away. What can I say? It's probably not a good idea for you to take me around other people because I'm not all that normal?

"Please, Addison? I'd really like you to be there."

He sounds so earnest and sweet that I can't help but agree to whatever he asks. I hesitantly accept his invitation and hope to God I haven't just made the biggest mistake of my life.

Chapter Eight
Comfortably Numb

"There's no shame in taking medication, Addison. Plenty of people need a little something to help with their depression. It doesn't mean you're weak. It just means you need a little boost. You've been on a small dose for a while now. Maybe it's time we bump it up a little bit," Dr. Thompson explains as she takes a sip of hazelnut coffee out of a mug that says "Let them eat cake."

I know it's normal and that one in ten people take some sort of antidepressant. I've read all of the literature, but that still doesn't mean I like it.

"For some people it's hard to get back on track after a tragedy. It's not going to turn you into a zombie or anything. It's just going to help keep your emotions in check so you aren't all over the place."

I trust Dr. Thompson as much as I *can* trust someone, and as I watch her write out a prescription refill for one hundred milligrams of Zoloft, I actually do feel a small weight lifted off of my shoulders. Maybe this will be the light at the end of the tunnel that I need. Maybe now my thoughts won't constantly be plagued with death and sadness.

As I pull the bottle of pills out of my medicine cabinet, I close the mirrored door and stand in front of the sink staring at myself. As I blindly open the lid and let one of the little blue pills spill into my hand, I wonder why I continue to do this. I've been taking this medication for a year now, and even though it keeps me from crying every single day and wanting nothing more than to curl up into a ball in bed and never get out, it hasn't helped. Instead, it does what Dr. Thompson said it wouldn't. It turns me into a zombie. I don't walk around in a daze or mumble incoherently, I just…don't. I don't feel; I don't care; I don't do anything other than get up every day and go through the motions. If I read a book that made other people sob for days, I feel nothing. If I watch a gut-wrenching movie, I stare at the screen and wonder what all the fuss was about. Nothing affects me and nothing shakes me.

Setting the bottle on the edge of the sink, I stare at the pill in my hand. Such a tiny little thing, the color of a robin's egg. It's so small and yet what it does to me is so huge.

I don't want to feel everything. I don't want to drown in my emotions, but I also don't want to keep going like this anymore. I want to feel something. I don't know what this thing with Zander is or where it's going, but I do know that it won't go anywhere if it's impossible for me to feel the emotions that go hand-in-hand with being with someone, especially someone like him. He's so full of life and I'm just blah.

Glancing up at my reflection in the mirror again, I wonder what it is he sees in me. My eyes are vacant and they have dark shadows under them, and I can't remember the last time I actually smiled when it wasn't forced. Why would he want to spend time with someone like me? I think he would have really loved the old me. The one who could always make people laugh and actually cared about things. The one who loved unconditionally and easily shared that love with others.

I've done as my dad said and took the last few days off from the bakery, but I honestly have no idea what to do with myself. I tried writing again, but the words wouldn't come. I tried reading but nothing held my interest. I even tried shopping, something a nineteen-year-old girl should love to do. I walked aimlessly around the mall and didn't buy anything.

Suddenly, it doesn't feel right to be taking this pill anymore. It doesn't feel right to shut everything off when I actually want to feel. There were definitely times when I should have been on this medication: when she was diagnosed, when she was sick, or even at her funeral. Maybe this little blue pill would have kept me together then instead of letting me fall apart.

I stood just outside the viewing room and stared at the open doorway, refusing to go in. My father was already there, choosing to go in alone. I could hear his sobs from out here as he stood over the casket.

I didn't want to go in there. I didn't want to see her like that, so still and quiet. She was never still OR quiet, and to see her like that now, in a perfectly pressed blue dress that she was going to wear to my high school graduation, makes me want to scream. I can hear the funeral director talking softly to my Aunt Katie behind me about how long the viewing will last and that if the family needed anything to let him know. I just wanted to tell him to shut up. What the family needed right now was her to be alive and not lying in a white casket with pink roses etched all around it. My mother hated roses. She would hate that people would be filing in here soon to stare at her and cry for her. She would hate that there were a hundred flower bouquets lined up all around the perimeter of the room she was in. All that money wasted on someone who would never get to enjoy them.

"Don't send me flowers when I'm dead. They're of no use to me when I'm gone. Give me flowers when I'm still here and can appreciate them."

A memory of the words she spoke each time we went to someone else's funeral and wandered around to look at all the arrangements filled my head and anger began to mix with the sadness.

I wanted to go in there, pick up all of the baskets and vases, and hurl them across the room. I wanted the cloying smell of roses and carnations and lilies gone from my nose. The smell made me sick to my stomach, and I knew that from now on, anytime I smelled a flower I would remember this moment.

"Come on, sweetie, it's time to go in. People are going to start showing up any minute now," Aunt Katie said softly as she walked up next to me and put her arm around my waist.

The funeral home had the close family members come in a half hour early so they could grieve in private for a little while before the masses showed up. Didn't they realize that thirty minutes was nowhere near long enough to grieve?

Aunt Katie gently pushed me forward and together we walked up to the open doorway. My father sat in the first row of chairs the funeral home had set up right in front of the casket. He had his head in his hands, and I could see his shoulders shaking with sobs. I didn't want to look, but I couldn't help it. My gaze slid across the deep red carpet by his feet, over to the black stand the casket rested on, and up the front of the shiny white marble with pink roses. The breath I'd been holding whooshed from my lungs when I saw her. It looked like her, but it didn't. In her hands she clutched a black rosary my father had given her for their anniversary a few years before. I remembered going to my grandfather's funeral when I was six years old and staring at his body, waiting to see his chest start moving with the breath of life again. I found myself doing that now. I stared at her chest and willed it to move. Please, God, let it move. Let this all be a nightmare. Please don't let it be real. My eyes traveled up to her face, and I had to swallow back a sob. She had on too much makeup. Why did they put lipstick on her? She never wore lipstick. I wanted to run up there and wipe it all off and tell her to open her eyes. I couldn't be here. I couldn't do this. It wasn't right and it shouldn't be happening.

Turning from my Aunt Katie's arms, I fled from the doorway, through the lobby, and down a hallway until I found the bathroom. I didn't turn on the light; I preferred the darkness right then. With heaving sobs I buried my face into the corner of the wall and cried. I cried so hard that my chest hurt.

"No, no, no, no, no," I sobbed over and over. "I don't want to go in there. I don't want to go in there. Why is this happening?"

My tears fell so fast they poured out of me and I let them. I didn't wipe them away or try to stop them. Maybe if I cried all of the tears I had in me it would wash away all of this pain. It would stop the hurt and make this all a bad dream. I didn't want to feel this anymore. I didn't want to feel anything anymore. I sank to my knees on the bathroom floor and cried for my mother and the unfairness of it all.

The memory fades and I quickly blink back tears, refusing to let them fall. Lifting my hand to my mouth, I pause right before popping the pill and look at myself in the mirror again. Who am I and what am I doing? What am I doing with my life and where am I going? Is this pill really the answer? Is shutting everything off really the solution to all of my problems? I don't want to feel everything, but I also don't want to feel nothing. I don't want to be a basket case, but I also don't want to be emotionless.

I take a deep breath and tip my hand over until the pill falls into the sink. Grabbing the bottle, I dump the rest of them until little blue pills are scattered all over the sink bowl. With a shaking hand, I reach over and turn on the faucet letting the cold water wash them all down the drain. When the last one disappears, I turn off the water, look back up at my reflection, and take a deep breath. I walk out of the bathroom and go over to my computer desk, powering up my laptop and logging onto Facebook. Going to her page, I stare at her profile picture. I click on *Account Settings* and then *Privacy*. My mouse hovers over *Deactivate Account*.

I should have deleted her page a long time ago. Every time I receive a notification for her birthday or see when other family members have posted messages about missing her I want to throw my computer across the room. Half of those people never even came to visit her when she was sick or called to see how she was, and now that she's gone, they suddenly miss her. They had all the time in the world to spend with her, but they were too busy with their own lives.

I know it's not healthy behavior to keep her account active, but I can't do it. I move the mouse away from the deactivation link and open a new message to her instead. Shutting down this account feels like saying good-bye to her all over again, and I'm not ready to do that. Maybe someday, but not now.

Dear Mom:

I wish I could talk to you again, just one more time.

I love you. I need you. I miss you.

Love,

Addison

Chapter Nine

Ghosts That We Knew

"I think you're making good progress, Addison. But you need to open yourself up to new experiences. You can't keep letting fear of the unknown stop you from living your life," Dr. Thompson explains.

"How am I supposed to do that? It's not that easy to just open myself up again when circumstances beyond my control have forced me to be closed off for so long," I complain.

"I know, but the good thing is you can recognize what you've been doing to yourself. You can easily admit that you've shut down your feelings and your emotions with other people for fear of getting hurt. It's a big step that you're able to do that, Addison, believe me."

I roll my eyes and laugh.

"The first step is admitting it? Are you really using the twelve steps on me right now?" I ask sarcastically.

"Why not? They don't just work for people with addiction problems. They can work for anyone who is struggling with something in their life. You've been struggling with depression, anger, sadness, trust...all of those things take time to get over, and all of those things require you to take certain steps toward overcoming those hurdles."

Dr. Thompson reaches over into the drawer of the table next to her and pulls out a sheet of paper and hands it to me.

"I'm sure you've gotten a copy of the twelve steps before at the support groups you've been to, but I want you to look at them again with fresh eyes. Think about how they can help *you*, instead of your father. You don't have to follow them word for word. The beauty of the twelve steps to recovery is that you can alter them to fit your needs. Step one: *We admit we are powerless over our addiction— that our lives have become unmanageable.* You felt powerless over the loss of your mother and what it did to your family, so you closed yourself off and your life became unmanageable."

I stare at the list, doing what she said and look at it with new eyes, reading the steps and trying to apply them to myself.

"Admitting how powerless you feel about your life is a big step towards healing, Addison. You can recognize the problems that forced you to become the person you are now, and you can begin moving forward. It's all about taking chances and living outside your comfort zone. You've become comfortable with the person you've become, but that doesn't mean it's the best thing for you or what's going to make you happy again. Step outside the wall you've built to protect yourself," she tells me as she reaches over to her side table and grabs her cup of hazelnut Panera coffee. I'm listening to everything she says, but all I can focus on is that stupid cup of coffee and I wonder if she drinks it week after week just to mess with me.

"I'm not saying you need to knock it down in one day so you're out there in the open, vulnerable to pain and fear. I'm saying just take a step around it. Poke your head out and if it gets to be too much, go back to the comfort of the wall. Eventually, if you step out from around it enough, you're going to realize that you don't need it anymore."

I reach up with a shaky hand to ring the doorbell and then rub my sweaty palms against the front of my jeans. Zander had offered to pick me up but I declined. I needed the quiet drive here to try and eliminate some of my nerves. I've spent every waking moment, since he sent me a text with the address to his parent's house, arguing with myself on whether or not I should come. Even though I can hear voices inside, and the chimes of the bell have already signaled my presence, I'm still trying to figure out how quickly I can jump off of the porch, start my car, and race out of here before anyone sees me.

The door flies open moments later, and Zander stands there in front of me in a long sleeve thermal shirt, worn jeans, and bare feet. His smile is contagious, and I quickly forget about running away as he grabs my hand and pulls me into the house.

The homey smell of multiple candles lit throughout the modern colonial hits me first and reminds me of my home growing up. We had an entire closet in the spare bedroom devoted to candles, and they were always all over the house. The warmth of Zander's hand as he pulls me closer to his side as we walk toward the loud voices and laughter makes me feel a little less tense about meeting his family.

As soon as we enter the large kitchen, I'm overwhelmed by greetings, hugs, and pats on the back from aunts, uncles, cousins, and siblings. They welcome me like I'm an old friend, and I wonder what Zander has told them about me. A fluttering of nerves flows through my stomach when I realize that he's obviously mentioned me to all of these people by now because they already know my name and gush over the fact that I work in a bakery. He talked about me to the people he cares about; he told them about me, and by the sound of it, he only told them the good parts. I'm pretty sure they wouldn't be so happy to meet me if they knew what a freak I've been around Zander since the day I met him and that I'm one step away from breaking down just by being in a room full of family that is so reminiscent of my own.

The way we used to be at least.

His mother is the last one to walk up to me, and she's the one I've been dreading the most to meet. Not because I think she'll judge me or instinctively know I'm not good for her son, although that thought has crossed my mind on more than one occasion this week, but because being around mothers is just hard for me. Seeing mothers and their children together fills me with such anger and jealousy that sometimes, no matter how hard I try, I can't keep those feelings at bay.

"Addison, it's so good to finally meet you. I'm Mary," she tells me warmly as she wraps her arms around me and engulfs me in a tight hug. I hold my breath as she cradles me to her, and I try not to think about how long it's been since someone did something as simple as hug me. "My son has done nothing but sing your praises. I've never seen him as happy as when he talks about you."

She pulls away and holds me at arm's length as she studies my face.

"Zander, you failed to mention how beautiful she is. I would kill to have her gorgeous eyes."

Zander laughs uncomfortably and playfully bumps his hip against his mother's. "Stop embarrassing me or I won't let you eat any cake."

I step back out of Mary's arms and shove my hands into the back pocket of my jeans as I watch their exchange while other family members flit about around the room, getting plates set at the table and joking easily with one another.

"My job in life is to embarrass you. Don't cross me or I'll bring out your baby albums," Mary tells him with a wag of her finger.

I bite down hard on my bottom lip to keep myself together. The way they talk and the way they interact reminds me so much of how my mom and I used to be, and it's unsettling.

Zander looks over at me, laughing at something else his mother says to him and immediately steps over to my side and wraps his arm around my waist, pulling me close.

"I think it's time to bring out my masterpiece so everyone can tell me what an awesome baker I am," he says loudly.

As his mother walks away from us and over to the fridge, Zander leans down close to my ear. "You okay?" he asks softly.

It's uncanny how well he knows me and can read me. It should make me nervous that someone I just met can see what I'm trying to hide, but it doesn't. With anyone else it probably would, but not with Zander. I plaster a smile on my face for his benefit and nod my head at him.

His arm slips from around my waist and he laces his fingers with mine, leading me over to the table where his mother has just set down a cake on a huge glass plate. At least, I think it's a cake. It sort of resembles a cake. It's covered in white frosting and has globs of pink frosting dotted all over it that I'm assuming are supposed to be flowers, but that's where the similarities end. The "cake" is leaning so far to one side that I honestly have no idea how it's even remaining upright. There are so many bumps and divots on the thing that I'm wondering if he just cut up a bunch of cupcakes and glued them together with frosting. I don't want to laugh, but it's really hard to hold it in. Everyone is standing around the table staring at this monstrosity with a straight face. His uncle bends down until his face is about two inches from it and cocks his head to the side like he's trying to figure out what it is.

"What the hell is that? It looks like something the cat yacked up!" Zander's eight-year-old brother, Luke, is the first to break the silence.

"Luke Andrew! Watch your mouth!" Mary scolds.

She tries to keep a straight face so her youngest son knows she means business, but it's no use. She immediately bursts out laughing, and when everyone else sees that it's okay, they all join in.

"Oh come on! It's not that bad!" Zander complains. This just makes everyone laugh even louder.

"I'm sorry we weren't able to make it to the decorating portion of our lesson the other night," I tell him with a giggle as his mom wipes tears of laughter from her eyes.

"Oh, honey, you are an amazing doctor, but a baker you are not!" Mary says with a laugh.

I glance quickly at Zander and see him wince a little at his mother's words.

"You're a doctor?" I ask him in shock. I immediately feel a little inadequate standing next to him. This is probably why I kept putting off asking him more about himself. I already knew he was a better person than me and this just proves it. Now I know why he always seems so together all the time. He's a freaking doctor. He's twenty-two years old and he's a doctor. Is that even possible? Is he a genius or something? He's probably been trying to diagnose me since we met. I can't help but feel a little betrayed by this knowledge even though it's my fault for never pursuing more information about him.

"No! I'm not a doctor," he quickly reassures me when he sees the obvious look of alarm on my face. "I'm an x-ray technician."

Mary scoffs and lightly shoves his shoulder. "Don't be so modest. It's much fancier than that. He's a specialist in rad-"

"Mom! Seriously, this is your birthday. For one day, you can hold off on bragging about me," Zander says with an uncomfortable laugh, effectively cutting her off. "Come on, everyone dig in. I swear it tastes better than it looks. I had a really good teacher."

He leans down and kisses the top of my head, and I close my eyes, savoring his closeness and pushing away the negative feeling of knowing yet another fact has been added to the growing list of things about Zander that make him more put together than I'll ever be.

Without hesitation, everyone grabs a plate while his mother slices up pieces of the leaning tower of cake. Some people sit at the table and others stand, but everyone eats the cake and agrees that it definitely tastes much better than it looks. The conversation flows easily, and I find myself being pulled into the happiness of their family and surprisingly have no problem talking and laughing with each of them. The ache in my heart at how many birthdays and holidays I spent exactly like this one isn't completely far from my thoughts, though. In the back of my mind is sadness and regret that my family fell apart so easily. The glue that held us all together is missing, and now we barely speak to one another, let alone gather in each other's houses like this to celebrate together.

"Oh, Zander, I forgot to ask you, did you hear about Tina Reddy's mom? They just found out she has Leukemia," Mary says sympathetically.

The bite of cake in my mouth goes down roughly, and I set my plate on the counter next to where I'm standing.

"You went to high school with Tina, didn't you?" his dad asks. "We just saw her parents a few months ago when we were out to dinner. Sad news."

Zander clears his throat uncomfortably and shifts his feet next to me.

"I guess it was a total shock. She's been feeling under the weather for a while and they ran some blood work. I feel so bad for that family. She's such a nice woman and now this. I should give them your cell number in case they have any—"

"Hey, we forgot to sing happy birthday," Zander says quickly.

The conversation about Tina Reddy's mom is forgotten as everyone gathers around Mary to sing, but the damage has already been done. I'm standing here in Zander's parent's kitchen thinking about that day a few years ago when we received similar news.

Mom had the flu for a little over a week now and when she called her doctor, he told her she might as well come in for some tests. "Better to be safe than sorry," he said. When I got out of school and finished with cheerleading practice, I sent her a text to see what was going on, and she said she was still at the hospital waiting for the doctor to come and talk to her. My dad ran to the bakery to close out the register for the end of the day, so she was sitting there alone, bored out of her mind.

When I got to the hospital, I went straight to the room number she sent me in the text and was surprised to see her in a hospital gown in bed.

"What are you doing getting all comfy and lazy? Shouldn't you be getting out of here soon?" I joked as I walked up to her bedside and gave her a kiss on the cheek.

"I have Leukemia." She blurted it out in a shocked voice, her face void of emotion.

"What?" I whispered as I pulled back so I could see her face.

Maybe I didn't hear her correctly or she misunderstood what the doctor said.

"The doctor just left. I'm going to be transported to Metro Hospital as soon as they can get an ambulance here."

She said it so calmly, like she was talking about the weather, not a life-threatening illness. While I was driving over there, blasting Top Forty radio and worrying about a stupid Spanish test I had the next day, my mother was getting these test results and she was all alone.

I wanted to curl up in bed with her and cry. Cancer was serious business. A lot of people received treatment and went on to lead healthy lives, but it was still scary. My mother was a rock and rarely got sick, aside from the occasional cold. This was big and it was bad, especially if they wanted to transport her to the largest hospital in the state that quickly. I couldn't get upset now, though. She needed me to be strong. She needed to know that I trusted the doctors to get her through this and that we would look back on this one day as just a bad moment in time, something easily forgotten.

"Okay, good. You'll go to Metro, start getting treatment, and then you'll be fine. Plus, you'll get to ride in an ambulance, hopefully with some really hot EMTs," I told her with a smile, pushing the worry I had for her as deep as it would go.

"They better be good-looking. The oncologist that was just in here is fugly," she told me with a laugh, reaching for my hand and squeezing it tight.

I clutched onto her and put on the bravest smile I could muster.

"I love you, Sweets," she told me softly.

"I love you too. Everything will be fine. You'll see."

The sound of singing comes to a close, and I force myself to join in on the last few bars of *Happy Birthday*.

"Oh my gosh, did you hear about Josh Mendleson?" Zander's uncle asks around a mouthful of cake.

"The town drunk? Has anyone *not* heard about what he did?" Mary says with a roll of her eyes.

"Wait, I must have missed this, what happened?" one of the cousins pipes in.

"That idiot should just live in rehab. Why they even let him out anymore is beyond me," Mary states bitterly. "He just got his fifth D.U.I. and threw a punch at the sheriff who pulled him over."

Groans echo around the table as I listen to them complain about a man who is the father of Loren Mendleson, someone I went to high school with. I only met the man once when I was in tenth grade and dropped Loren off after school. I don't know much about him, but he sounds like he could be my father's twin. I have to force myself to not show any reaction to the words they're saying.

"What a waste of space that guy is. How can someone turn into such a loser like that? Can you imagine being in his family? They are probably completely mortified. I don't know how they can even show their faces around town. They should just move.

There's obviously no hope for him. He's going to keep screwing up, and his family is going to pay the price," Zander's dad says with disgust.

I wasn't that close with Loren in school, but I know what she's probably feeling, and it isn't mortification. She doesn't care that the whole town is talking about her father over cake. She cares that her life is most likely spiraling out of control and she has no way of stopping it because of her father's actions. She looks at the person who raised her and loved her and wonders why he would do something like that and hurt everyone in his life. She wonders why he didn't love her enough to stay sober. I suddenly want to knock on Loren's door and tell her I understand, but most of all, I want to get out of this room and away from the talk of town drunks. It hurts to hear people I just met and genuinely liked judging someone they know nothing about. It breaks my heart to think that if they knew half the things my father has said and done, they'd look at me differently and judge *me*.

It was bad enough having to think about the day my mother was diagnosed with Leukemia, but this is too much. I suddenly feel claustrophobic being in this room, like the walls are closing in on me and I'm running out of air. I turn and walk quickly from the room, ignoring Zander's voice as he calls to me. When I'm out of view of the kitchen, I take off running through the house until I reach the front door, throwing it open and charging out into the warm sunshine. I run down the steps of the front porch and out into the middle of the yard, stopping when I get far enough away from the house that I can breathe. Wrapping my arms around my stomach, I hold myself together as I turn my face up to the sun and close my eyes, letting the bright rays warm my face and heat up the coldness that washed through me while standing in Zander's parent's kitchen.

I had stuck my head out beyond the wall, just like Dr. Thompson suggested, and now I just want to run back behind it. I want to crawl back to the other side where I know no one can hurt me with their words and actions; where I can listen to people complain about drunks and not let it affect me; where I can hang out with a happy family and not hate what's become of my life because I don't have that anymore.

Dr. Thompson lied. As soon as I left the comfort of my wall, the bricks I carefully put in place began crumbling. As soon as I took one step forward and let Zander in, there was nothing left of my protection but a pile of dust and debris.

Chapter Ten

Lego House

"I know we've touched on this before, but in light of everything that's been going on lately, do you feel like the new individuals in your life are people you can talk to when you're feeling particularly down or confused about a situation? Do you now feel like you have someone in your life that will listen and support you?" Dr. Thompson asks me.

A sharp pain shoots through my chest, and I rub at the ache with the heel of my hand when I think about how easy it would have been to answer these questions a year ago. I wouldn't have had to even contemplate trusting new people because the old ones were all I ever needed.

"Addison? Do you feel like you have a solid support group surrounding you now?" Dr. Thompson asks me again, bringing my focus back to her. I move my gaze away from the Snowbabies figurine she's using as a paperweight on her desk and look at her.

"I don't know anything about them, so I don't know if I trust them or not. I feel close to Meg because we've been through similar issues, and something about Zander makes me feel comfortable and like I *could* trust him, but I just don't know. I don't know if I want to trust him. I don't know if I *can* trust him...I just don't know anything," I complain.

"I know you've had a rough year, especially with those that you were closest to. Why don't you tell me a little bit about how you feel those people let you down," she asks, crossing her legs and folding her hands in her lap.

"I had a lot of close friends and one girl I called my best friend. I haven't heard from them since the funeral, though. The week she died they called every single day to check on me," I told her, picking at my cuticles. "My aunt told me at the funeral that even though she could never take the place of my mother, she would still call and check up on me every single day and tell me that she loved me. She called twice. I haven't spoken to her in months."

I grit my teeth in an effort to keep the tears from falling. It's easier to deal with resentment than sadness.

"I can hear the irritation in your voice. Does it make you angry that your friends and your aunt haven't called? Haven't checked in to see how you are?" she asks as she makes notes on the legal pad in her lap.

I shrug without looking up at her. "I guess. I mean that's how it goes though, isn't it? The same thing happened with all the other family members. Once the main event was over, they went back to work, back to school, back to doing whatever it was they were busy with before it happened, and they just moved on. It doesn't occur to them that there are people who aren't able to do that."

Dr. Thompson puts her pencil down and we make eye contact. "And you're one of those people."

It's a statement, not a question. She knows why I'm here and what I did to stop the pain so there's no reason to be obtuse.

"It's very hard when you don't have people to rely on. People you can call when you're feeling sad or lonely."

Her words make my eyes sting, and a lump forms in my throat that is impossible to swallow. Most people probably wouldn't understand the bond my mother and I shared. Daughters typically hate their mothers through most of their teenage years and sometimes into early adulthood, but I never did. Maybe it was because I was her only child, or maybe it was because it was so difficult for her to get pregnant with me. Whatever the reason, we had a relationship that many envied. Our bond was forged through years of it just being the two of us. My father had always worked the night shift. By the time I woke up in the morning, he was already asleep after working twelve hours. My mother and I did everything together. She took me everywhere, did everything with me, and there wasn't anything we couldn't talk about.

Everyone has at least one individual in their life that they know will always be there for them no matter what. They will be your rock, your shoulder to cry on, someone to laugh with and confide in, and someone who will call you on your bullshit and tell it to you straight. My mother was absolutely that person for me. And my person is gone and never coming back.

"I want you to do me a favor before next week, Addison. I want you to confide in someone. Whether it's Meg or Zander, it doesn't matter. I want you to reach out to one of them and tell them what you're feeling. Talk to them. Give them a chance to earn your trust and support you. This can correspond with Step Five: *Admit to God, to ourselves, and to another human being the exact nature of our wrongs.* And remember, we're tailoring this to meet your needs. So, admit to another person the exact nature of what you're struggling with."

After standing in the middle of the front yard for several minutes, I move over to the shade of a huge oak tree. I sit down at the base of it, crossing my legs in front of me, and begin picking individual blades of grass and tearing them down the middle. I have a nice pile going in my lap when a shadow falls over me. I don't pause in my methodical hand mowing of the grass as he sits down next to me and leans his back against the trunk of the tree.

"Soooooo, what's new?" Zander asks in a singsong voice, breaking the silence after a few minutes.

I can't help but laugh at the casual way he asks that question. I just ran out of his parent's home in a snit without saying a word to anyone. If they didn't know it before, they sure as hell know now that I'm a freak with issues.

"Oh, nothing much. Just tending to your parents' lawn. It's gotten a little overgrown," I reply as I finally look up and meet his eyes.

The thing I like most about Zander is that I never see any judgment in them—just understanding and kindness.

"I've been meaning to talk to them about that. Lawn mowers are so last year. What they really need is someone to hand pick their yard."

I stare at him quietly for several long minutes. He reaches over and gently brushes my bangs out of my eyes, his fingers trailing down the side of my cheek before cupping my chin and holding it in place. He places a soft kiss on the tip of my nose, and I blink back tears when he pulls away and lets his hand drop to mine, stopping my manic grass pulling. He tugs my hand over to his own lap and flips it over so my palm is up.

"I'm twenty-two years old and I make a living taking pictures of people's insides," he begins speaking as he lightly traces the lines on my palm with his fingertips. "I have an eight-year-old brother who has no filter and a fifteen-year-old brother who has no morals. I'm obviously the best big brother in the world, and they both look up to me immensely."

I chuckle a little as he verbally pats himself on the back and continues on.

"I've lived a pretty good life, and sometimes that makes people think everything has been easy for me. I'm not saying I have a dark, hidden past or anything, but my life hasn't always been roses," he explains with a shrug. "I struggle every day to be honest and to not hurt the people I care about. It's a fine line between doing what's right and doing what you think is best. My mother likes to call me a know-it-all, and sometimes it gets me in trouble. My dad cheated on my mom a few years ago, and it's been a bumpy road. They worked everything out and things between them are better than they've ever been, but I'm still struggling with hating him for what he did. It's exhausting to hate and love someone equally."

My heart stutters as he laces his fingers through mine and pulls my hand up to his mouth, placing a kiss on the top of it.

"I know we haven't known each other long, but I hope you realize by now that I'm not a stalker," he says with an easy smile. "I like you. I care about you. And I want you to trust me."

How can I *not* trust him? He opened up his whole world to me by letting me meet his family and telling me personal things about himself. He did all of this without me asking. It's like he instinctively knew I needed something from him so I could feel comfortable enough to do the same.

"My father and I have had a rough time of it lately. He fell apart one day, and he's been in and out of rehab so many times

I've lost count," I ramble. I speak so fast that all of my words run together, and I don't really know if anything I'm saying makes sense, but Zander sits there quietly and listens—just listens. I realize suddenly that it's something I've needed for a long time, someone to just listen. It's different with a therapist. They're paid to listen to you. When it's someone who is in your life for the sole reason of just wanting to be near you, it means so much more.

"You sort of met my father the other night. He got out of rehab early, and it scares me to death. I don't want to go through this again with him. I've gotten so used to picking up his pieces, and I'm just exhausted. I don't want to do it anymore. I don't know *how* to do it anymore when I feel like I can't even pick up my own pieces."

I finally stop talking and take a deep breath, looking away from Zander and over at his house where one big happy family is gathered. I hope he knows just how lucky he really is.

"Wait here for just one second, okay?" he asks, getting up off of the grass quickly. "I have something I want to show you."

I nod my head in reply, and he's about to leave but stops suddenly. He turns back around, squats down, and kisses me. His lips press gently against mine, and then they're gone all too quickly. When he kisses me, I forget about my problems and the world around me disappears. I want to feel his lips on me again so I can close my eyes and just forget.

"Two seconds," he tells me again with a smile before jumping up and racing into the house.

He's back before I can even wonder what he's doing and whether or not I freaked him out by blurting that information about my dad to him. He walks across the yard carrying a small, blue plastic case with a Lego sticker on the side of it.

Flopping down on the grass next to me, he takes the lid off of the box, tips it over, and dumps Lego pieces all over the ground. He starts rummaging through the pile, collecting a few pieces and snapping them together.

"Um, what are we doing?" I ask in confusion as he hands me the small tower of yellow, red, and blue Legos that he quickly put together.

"Luke let me borrow these. We're building a Lego house," he tells me nonchalantly, like it's the most natural thing in the world for two young adults to be doing out in the front yard after they both just spilled their guts to each other.

"A house? We don't have directions. How are we going to build a house?" I ask as I look in the box for one of those Lego booklets with step-by-step instructions and don't find one. Figuring Zander thinks building Legos in the front yard is normal, I decide I might as well just go with it.

"One of the best things about Legos is that you don't need instructions. Sometimes, they don't even come with instructions, and you just have to work your way through the mess to figure out how everything should work."

I flip the tower of Legos around and around in my hand as Zander digs through the pile on the grass and quickly snaps together a square of Legos that resemble the walls of a house. He reaches for a large blue one and tries to make it fit in a corner, but it doesn't work.

"And if something doesn't fit, if one of your pieces just isn't working, you can put it aside and find another one. There are so many pieces to work with that you don't have to try and force one in where it doesn't belong. You may not need that piece right now, and it may not be helping you right at this moment, but that doesn't mean it isn't important and won't fit somewhere else down the line when you need it more."

He finds a yellow piece that works in the corner, and before long he's built a tiny little house complete with a swinging door and a roof.

"We've got a lot of Legos left over," I tell him, dipping my hand into the pile and letting them fall back to the ground a few pieces at a time.

"You don't have to try and pick up all of the pieces at once, sometimes you only need to use a few of them at a time. If you try and pick them all up and use them all at the same time, it's overwhelming and frustrating when you start to drop them or you just can't make them work."

Trying to press another piece on top of the roof for a makeshift chimney, he pushes too hard and a few of the pieces of the wall break off and fall to the ground.

"Oh crap. You just broke our house," I tell him with a laugh as I reach over and grab the pieces that fell off.

He takes them from my hand and snaps them back into place.

"Another good thing about Legos. If it falls apart, it doesn't mean it's destroyed. It just means you have to pick up the pieces and start again."

He's looking at me instead of the Lego house when he says those words and now I understand the point of all of this. He's trying to tell me that I'm not broken. That no matter what my problems are, they don't have to break me.

"You can still pick up the pieces, Sugar. They fell apart for a little while, but it doesn't mean anything is damaged. Everything can be fixed. And you don't have to fix it alone. There's always someone who will help you rebuild."

I don't bother to try and stop the tears that pool in my eyes this time. I've kept myself closed off for so long that I'm actually surprised at how easy it is to cry. I feel the first tear slide down my cheek, and I don't bother to wipe it away. Zander scoots closer to me and moves my head down to his shoulder. He wraps both of his arms around me and pulls us back against the trunk of the tree and just holds me while I softly cry into his neck. It's frightening to open myself up so completely with someone. It's like closing your eyes and jumping off of a cliff, not knowing whether or not there will be a safety net at the bottom to catch you.

Right now, wrapped in Zander's arms as the sun slowly sets behind his parents' house, with a multicolored Lego house next to us that was broken and put back together again, I wonder if I've just found my safety net.

Chapter Eleven

Landslide

"I think you're doing remarkably well considering everything," Dr. Thompson tells me, raising one eyebrow at me when she catches me picking at my nails. "You've taken a step back from your responsibilities and you're finally learning to live again."

I look away from her and stare at a black rosary that sits on the table next to her chair. I've never seen it before and wonder why it's there now. I hadn't realized she was Catholic, but I guess that isn't really a surprise since we're not here to talk about her. I tear my gaze away from the pile of beads to look back at her.

"I know you can get back to the girl you used to be. You just have to want it bad enough. People change as they get older, but parts of who they used to be are still in there and they carry that with them. Your sense of humor, your appreciation of life...those are all things that are still inside of you. They've just been dormant for so long you don't know how to find them. You can't let other people dictate what type of person you are. It's up to you to be who you want to be. Who do you want to be, Addison?"

I sit there for several long minutes and contemplate her words. I want to be *me* again. I want to look forward to the future and enjoy the simple things in life. I want to have friends again, and I want to be able to confide in someone without worrying about what they will think of me. I want to remember what it's like to not have a care in the world or anxiety about what the next day will bring. I want so many things. I'm just not sure if I'm strong enough to get them.

"No, Luke, we are not going for ice cream. You haven't even eaten lunch yet," Zander tells his little brother as we get out of the car at the park.

Luke grumbles his complaint as we wander over to the swing set and each of us grabs a swing.

To my surprise, I still haven't scared Zander away. We've spent every day together since his mother's birthday last weekend. He even helped me at the bakery one night when my dad had a meeting to go to. He dropped a tray of cupcakes and burned his arm on the oven, but he still swore he had the best time ever. I'm hoping it was because of how many times we snuck back into the kitchen to kiss. While Zander and Luke argue over the benefits of ice cream before lunch, I gently swing myself back and forth and think about how he wrapped his arms around me that night and lifted me up to sit on the island in the kitchen. I remember what it felt like to wrap my legs around his waist while he used his fingertips to touch every inch of my face as if he was memorizing it. When I close my eyes, I can still feel his hands inch under my shirt and the warmth of his palms as he moved them up over my ribcage to my breasts. Butterflies flutter through my stomach when I think about how badly I want his hands on me again. He's so gentle and sweet with me. He always asks before he does anything to make sure I'm okay with it. I'm not used to having someone so concerned for my well-being and it feels nice. It's good to have someone looking out for me for once.

"Zander, guess what Leah at school can do," Luke says, cutting off my thoughts as I watch him dig his heels into the dirt to stop swinging.

"No clue, buddy. What can she do?" Zander asks him as we both watch Luke jump down off of his swing and stand in front of us.

"She can do this."

He jumps up in the air kicking his legs out at odd angles and then loses his footing when he comes back down landing on his butt in the grass.

"Wow. I have no idea what that was. But if she can do that, she must be pretty cool," Zander jokes.

"It was a toe touch, duh," Luke says with a roll of his eyes as he stands up and wipes the dirt off of his jeans.

"That wasn't a toe touch," I tell him, standing up from my swing and going over next to him. "This, is a toe touch."

Raising both of my arms straight above my head, I take a deep breath, swing them back a little to build up my momentum, and then leap into the air, easily spreading my legs and touching my toes before coming back down and landing smoothly.

Both boys are staring at me with their mouths open and their eyes wide.

"Dude, you just did the splits in the air," Luke says in awe. "How did you do that?"

I shrug my shoulders like it's no big deal, because it isn't. I used to do those things in my sleep after eight years of cheerleading and eleven years of gymnastics.

"That was nothing," I tell him with a wink. "This might be a little cooler."

Stepping a few feet away from him, I put my feet together and my arms straight out in front of me, glancing over my shoulder quickly to make sure nothing is behind me. Swinging my arms down by my sides and bending my knees, I throw my body backwards until I'm flipping upside down in a perfect back handspring. My hands hit the ground first, then my feet follow and I stand up straight, unable to keep the smile off of my face. I can't even remember the last time I did this. It was probably the day before my mother died when I went to my last cheerleading practice ever.

"Oh my gosh, you HAVE to teach me how to do that so I can tell Leah to suck it!" Luke exclaims.

"LUKE!" Zander scolds. "Go over and play on the monkey bars for a while."

Luke huffs and kicks at a rock with the toe of his shoe. "Fine. I'll go for now, but I'll be back and you are going to teach me how to be awesome like you."

I laugh as he races away from us and over to the jungle gym.

"Well, there you have it. You are officially awesome," Zander says with a laugh as I walk over to him and sit back down on the swing next to him.

"It's good to know someone thinks so," I tell him with a smile as I push myself with my feet.

"Don't worry, he's not the only one. I happen to think you're pretty awesome myself. And my parents won't stop asking me when I'm going to bring you over again."

Tilting my head back and looking up at the sky as I swing, I take a deep breath of the spring air and feel peaceful for the first time in a long time. I'm not worried about my father, or the bakery, or how much I miss my mom. My only concern right now is wishing I could bottle this feeling and keep it with me forever.

"So now you've got me curious. Where did you learn how to do that stuff?" Zander asks.

Pulling my gaze away from the clouds, I look down at him and think about the person I used to be and what Dr. Thompson told me.

"You may find this hard to believe, but I used to be a cheerleader," I tell him.

"Why would I find that hard to believe?"

I shrug and lean my head against the chains that hold the swing.

"I'm not exactly the peppiest person in the world. People don't look at me and think, 'Now that girl's got a lot of spirit.' But they used to. I was loud and energetic and I loved to make people laugh," I tell him pensively.

"So what changed?"

His voice is soft and he turns himself in his swing so he's facing me.

"A lot of things I guess. One disaster after another until I just didn't care anymore. I didn't care if I was happy. I just cared about making it through each day."

We swing side-by-side in silence for a little while before he asks another question.

"Did you always want to work at the bakery?"

I shake my head as I watch Luke scaling the monkey bars off in the distance.

"I never wanted to work there. The bakery and I have a love/hate relationship. I love it because it reminds me of being younger, but I hate it for the same reasons. I'm only working there because I have to until my dad can finally get it together. If he doesn't, I guess I'll be working there until I die," I tell him, attempting to make a joke out of something that depresses me just thinking about it. That bakery was never my dream. It's depressing to think that I might spend the rest of my life living someone *else's* dream instead of my own.

"If you didn't have to work there, what would you be doing?" Zander asks.

I don't even have to think about my answer. I tell him the first thing that always comes to mind whenever anyone used to ask me this question.

"I'd be in college studying English and writing a book in my spare time."

I can feel his eyes on me, and I glance over at him to see a huge smile on his face.

"A writer, huh? That's pretty cool. Have you written anything before?" he asks.

"I've written a ton of things over the years. Poems, short stories, a couple of plays… It's probably all complete crap which is why I should go to school for it. I don't know. There's just something about sitting down and creating a story from scratch. Imagining another time, another place, and putting yourself there. Making the characters do and say exactly what you want them to and having the story unfold exactly how you planned. Nothing else exists but that story. You can shut out the world around you and just live in this make-believe place.

People don't have to die or drink too much. You can turn the story into anything you want. I'll take a story over real life any day."

I realize I've been rambling and quickly force myself to stop. When I think about my writing, I always get worked up and I can talk about it for days.

"Will you let me read something you've written?" Zander asks.

"You wouldn't want to read anything I've written, believe me," I tell him with a laugh, thinking about all of the notebooks filled with sappy love poems and romance stories stashed in my closet.

"I beg to differ. I would love to read anything you wrote because it came from you. It came from your heart and your soul and it would be amazing," he tells me, bringing his swing to a stop and angling towards me.

Reaching his arms out, he wraps his hands around the chains of my swing and pulls me over to him until my legs are in between his own.

"If you could only write one story, one story that everyone would read, what would you want it to be about?" he asks as he stares into my eyes.

"My life," I whisper. "Does that sound narcissistic? Writing a book about myself?"

He shakes his head at me and smiles. "Nope, not at all. It's life. It's the bumps and the bruises, the pain and the fear; it's messy and it's real and it's not some perfect little story that can be tied up in a bow. It's exactly what you should write about. And I damn well better be the first one who gets to read it."

I laugh at him and do something I've wanted to do since we first got here. I lean forward and press my lips to his. Sliding one hand around the back of his neck, I run my fingers through his hair and hold his head against mine. While he grips tightly to the chains of my swing to hold me in place, I take my time kissing him and touching his face.

"Eeeeew, you guys are gross. You know you can get cooties that way, right?" Luke complains from right behind us.

We break apart slowly and laugh at his disgust.

Zander lets go of the chains and I swing away from him.

"Why aren't you busy playing?" Zander asks Luke.

"I'm bored. I don't have anyone to play with."

Jumping off of my swing, I grab Zander's hand and pull him up, walking us over to where Luke stands.

"I have an awesome idea. Something we can all do together," I tell him.

"Are you going to teach me how to flip?" he asks excitedly.

"Not yet," I tell him. "That's something you need to work up to."

Grabbing Zander by his arms, I position him so he's standing right next to Luke, and then I move right in front of them so we're facing each other.

"Okay, boys, hands on your hips," I instruct.

They do as I say and I try not to laugh at how serious and cute they both look. Luke is like a miniature version of Zander with dark hair and light eyes.

"Repeat after me. Go, fight, win."

They both say the words together, and when Luke messes up and starts to say them a second time, Zander shoves him in the shoulder, and Luke punches him back in the arm.

"Wow, that really sucked. I couldn't hear you at all," I teasingly admonish them.

They don't hesitate to scream the words as loud as they possibly can, and Luke starts coughing because of how high-pitched his voice goes.

"You both need some work, but we're moving on. Bring both of your arms up above your head in the shape of a V, like this..." I show them, making fists with my hands and raising my arms above my head.

Luke copies my movements immediately, but Zander stands there staring at me.

"Wait, are you teaching us how to *cheer*?" he asks in shock. "We're dudes. We don't cheer."

Lowering my arms, I saunter over to him until I'm right up against his chest, going up on my tiptoes and sliding my breasts against him as I move. I place one palm on his chest and lean to the side, placing my lips right against his ear.

"Pretty please, Zander? It would make me really happy," I whisper, letting my lips gently graze his ear.

I pull back away from him, and he clears his throat and swallows thickly.

"Whatever the lady wants, the lady gets," he says in a daze as I smile at him and skip back to my spot in front of them.

I spend the rest of the afternoon teaching them cheers and showing Zander a little bit of who I used to be. I feel carefree, flirty, and happy. I've missed this part of myself so much. I've missed being able to let go and just live.

"Thanks for taking Luke to the park with me," Zander tells me as he holds my hand and we make our way to his car after giving into Luke and stopping off for ice cream on the way home.

"Thanks for inviting me. I had a good time."

As Luke clamors into the backseat and busies himself with his seatbelt, Zander pulls me against him and leans my back against the passenger door.

He stares at me without saying anything for so long that I finally can't take it and break the silence.

"What?'

He slowly smiles at me before resting his forehead against my own. "I'm just glad you're here," he tells me quietly.

"Me too," I whisper back.

And for the first time, I truly mean it. If I went through with my plans a year ago, I would have missed out on all of these moments with him. They are becoming important and special to me, and so is he.

I can almost feel some of the weight lifting off of my shoulders. I can practically see some of my worries floating away, and it feels right. It feels like it's time to finally let go of some of the pressure I've put on myself.

Chapter Twelve
Let You Down

"You can't control everything, Addison," Dr. Thompson tells me. "Sometimes things just happen and you aren't responsible for them. I know it's hard when you want answers and you don't get them."

No matter how many times she's told me this, it's still difficult for me to understand. I want to know why my mother had to go so suddenly. I want to know why my dad couldn't be strong. I want to know why it's so hard for me to move forward.

"You just need to remember that none of this is your fault. Your father is an adult and makes his own choices. He didn't become an alcoholic because he didn't love you enough; he did it because he didn't love *himself* enough. That's the hardest thing for families of addicts to understand. It's not because of anything you did or didn't do. You've had a lot of responsibilities piled on your young shoulders, and it sounds like your father is trying to make up for that. He's trying to be a better person and prove that to you. Open yourself up to the possibility that maybe he's finally ready to be the person you need. You can't *make* him want to be sober. You can't control the decisions he makes. All you can do is live your own life and do what you can to make *yourself* happy again."

As the time winds down on our weekly session, I wonder once again if it's that simple. In my mind I know I can't control the actions of others, but it's still hard not to feel responsible sometimes.

"I know your faith used to be very important to you and that you've lost a little bit of it along the way. Maybe it's time to start utilizing that cheesy slogan you hate so much. 'Let go and let God.' I know we're doing these a little out of order, but sometimes that's how it works. Step two: *Come to believe that a power greater than ourselves can restore us to sanity.* Hand over the reins, Addison. Let Him worry about the future and all the what-ifs. Just let go."

My dad has been back home for a few weeks now and surprisingly has spent every single day at the bakery. Unless he has a meeting or an appointment with his doctor, every time I come in, he grabs me by the shoulders, turns me around, and sends me right back out the door. The good news is I've had more time to spend with Zander. The bad news is I spend the majority of that time worrying about things at the store and wondering if everything is okay.

"Maybe I should call one more time before we leave," I tell Zander as I pace behind him while he loads a picnic basket and blanket into the trunk of his car. I don't worry too much when I'm just going to be out of cell phone range for a few hours, but today we're going up into the mountains to hike and have a picnic. That's an entire day of being away where he won't be able to call me if something goes wrong.

"We have a huge cupcake order for the Marshall wedding that's being picked up today, and I need to make sure—"

"Sugar, I'm sure everything is fine. You're dad knows what he's doing," Zander interrupts reassuringly as he closes the trunk.

I let out a huge sigh as he turns around to face me. He brings his hands around my waist, clasping his hands together against my lower back, and pulls me up against his chest. My hands slide up the front of his shirt until my right hand rests flat against his heart, and I can feel it beating, steady and sure, under my palm.

"I know it's hard to let go and put your faith in him, but he's been doing good so far, right?"

I nod my head in resignation and run my hands the rest of the way up the front of him and settle my arms on top of his shoulders. We've spent a lot of time together lately. We've done everything from dinner, movies, going for coffee, and building more Lego houses to just sitting on his front porch together watching the sun set. After he drops me off at my apartment each night, we spend hours texting each other back and forth, just talking about our lives. I know he always wanted to work in a hospital helping people because his grandfather had severe diabetes and his family spent a lot of time visiting him when Zander was younger. He loved how even when someone was gravely ill, the sight of a favorite nurse, doctor, or another hospital worker could brighten them up and put a smile on their face. I know he takes being a big brother very seriously. Even though he no longer lives at home, he spends a lot of time with his brothers, together and individually, giving them advice and making sure they stay on the right track.

I know so much about him, and I feel comfortable with him, but there's something in the back of my mind warning me that maybe we're moving too fast. Maybe we're *too* comfortable with each other too soon. There are still two very important parts of myself that I haven't shared with him yet: my mother and that day at the cemetery. I know I need to tell him. I know I need to lay it all on the line so he knows what he's gotten himself in to, but I just can't do it yet. I know that's the moment when I'll finally see the understanding in his eyes replaced by pity and maybe even disgust. I'm not ready for that yet. I'm not ready for him to look at me any differently. His support and friendship mean too much to me right now to taint them with any more of my problems and history. I'll tell him; I *have* to tell him. Just not right now.

"Let's just go have a nice picnic in the mountains, and then if you're good, I'll let you go to the shop and check on your dad," Zander says with a wink and a smile.

He tightens his hold on me and my breath catches in my throat. It's the same thing every time I'm this close to him. The feel of his body pressed up against mine sends a rush of excitement and tingles through my belly that make me want to forget all about our plans and just spend the day alone with him in bed. We haven't done much more than kiss and some light exploration with our hands, but each time it makes me feel alive and wanted, and I know he's the one I want to give everything to. He's the only one who has ever made me feel this way, and I know it won't be long before I give over another piece of myself to him that I've never given to another man. Every time we're alone he makes sure to tell me that he doesn't want to pressure me into anything and that it's up to me how far we go. I know it's insane to want to give him something this significant and special when I haven't even given him the most important part: the truth. I know taking this step with him is a way to make myself feel alive again and that shouldn't be the reason I want to move forward with him, but I can't help it. More than anything, I just want to feel something other than dead inside. And I *will* give him the truth. Maybe once I take this next step with him, it will give me the strength and courage I need to finally come clean.

As his lips brush against mine and I run my fingers through his hair and deepen the kiss, I know that my mind is already made up about just how far we'll go and how soon it will happen.

The ringing of my cell phone in my back pocket forces us apart, and I chuckle at Zander as he takes a few steps away and adjusts himself in his jeans, taking a few deep, calming breaths. I can't help but feel giddy knowing that I have that effect on him.

The smile on my face as I watch Zander quickly dies when I hear the panic in my dad's voice.

"Addison, have you talked to Meg today? She hasn't shown up for work and she's not answering her phone," he tells me in a frazzled voice. I can hear the clanging of pots and pans in the background and the hum of customers giving their orders.

"No, I haven't spoken to her in a few days," I tell him. A wave of guilt washes through me when I realize I haven't even seen her in a week since my dad continues to banish me from the bakery.

"Do you need me to come up there?" I ask him as Zander comes over to stand next to me and gives me a questioning look.

"Meg didn't show up for work and my dad hasn't heard from her," I whisper to him as my dad curses loudly into the phone after I hear a crash of something falling to the floor.

"No, I've got it under control. I don't want to ruin your day," he reassures me.

"Why don't we drive over to her place and check on her?" Zander asks.

I nod at him and mouth a silent "thank you" and let my dad know what we're doing and that I'll get back to him before ending the call.

"I'm sorry. I'm ruining our picnic lunch."

Zander takes my hand and leads me over to the passenger side of his car and opens the door for me.

"Nonsense. Nothing is ruined. We'll go check on her and then continue on with our amazingly romantic lunch in the park where I can rest my head on your lap and you can feed me grapes and tell me how awesome I am," he tells me with a wink.

I get into the car with a roll of my eyes and a laugh as he closes my door. I hope that I can have a million more days exactly like this.

"Meg, come on, open up," I yell through the door.

We've been standing outside of her apartment pounding on the door for five minutes, and she has yet to answer.

"I know you're in there. I saw your car out front."

Zander casually leans his shoulder against the wall next to the door and crosses his arms over his chest. "Want me to check with the super and see if he can let us in?"

I sigh in frustration and continue staring at the door, willing it to open.

"I don't know. She's probably just in there sleeping with her ear buds in and her iPod cranked as loud as it will go. She'll kick my ass if we just walk in on her."

I pull up her number again on my phone, and just as I get ready to hit send and call her for the fifth time, we hear a loud crash and the sound of breaking glass from inside. Zander quickly pushes off the wall and moves next to me.

"Stand back, Sugar," he tells me, and I get behind him.

With a powerful thrust of his leg, he kicks in the door and it flies open, banging against the inside wall of her apartment. Rushing around him, I race inside shouting Meg's name as I go.

"MEG! WHERE ARE YOU? MEG!"

Zander is close on my heels and bumps into the back of me when I come to a dead stop in her bedroom doorway.

"Meg? Oh Jesus, what the hell?"

I can't force my feet to move even though I need to.

No, no, no. Please, God, no. She wouldn't do this again. She wouldn't.

I need to go to her and check on her, but I can't. My friend is crumpled in a ball on the floor of her room, surrounded by broken glass, and there's blood covering her arms in several different places, and I can't make myself go to her.

Zander pushes past me and races to her side, crouching down next to her, not even caring that he's stepping and kneeling in glass and blood.

"Hey there, sunshine, wake up. Come on, look at me, wake up," Zander tells her softly as he puts both of his hands on either side of her face and turns her head towards him.

I don't even realize I'm holding my breath until her eyes slowly blink open and she smiles up at him.

"Hey there, hot stuff," she slurs weakly.

Something's not right. Aside from the obvious, she's lying in a pile of broken lamps, picture frames, and God knows what else, her voice is off. I glance quickly around the room and my gaze zeroes in on several empty prescription bottles on top of her bed.

"Addison, call 9-1-1," Zander tells me quietly as he gently moves Meg's hair out of her eyes with his fingers.

I hear him, but I can't do anything other than stare at the bottles of pills. I count three bottles, and I don't see any stray pills anywhere. Did she take them all? What did she take? Why would she do this? I know she's done this before. Jesus! We met in the psych ward of the hospital with matching wrist bandages to cover our matching vertical scars, but she's fine now. We're both fine now. We're both living our lives and know that single weak moment in time was a one-shot-deal. We aren't going to do it again because we don't really want to die.

But maybe that's not true. I know it's true for me, but what about her? It's not like we ever talked about things like that with each other. Our friendship was based on not prying into each other's lives, and it worked.

As I stare at Zander while he softly talks to Meg and tries to keep her awake and focused on him, I realize that it didn't work. It never worked. It was a stupid idea, and it's not what friendship is about at all. Friendship is about being there for someone else, helping them through the hard times and celebrating the good times with them. It's about knowing everything about the other person and still loving them and sticking by their side. I didn't do any of this with Meg. I kept her at a distance and had no idea what she went through, what she was *still* going through. Standing here watching her struggle to keep her eyes open, I'm thrown back in time to the day I walked into my parent's home after my dad's frantic phone call.

I raced into the house and ran into my aunt in my parent's kitchen.

"Stay here, sweetie. The coroner is back in the bedroom right now," *she told me, resting her hands on my shoulders.*

I shrugged them off and tried to move past her.

"I need to go back there. I need to see her."

She wrapped her arms around me from behind and held me against her as I struggled to be free. I needed to get down the hallway; I needed to see that this was all a joke. It couldn't be real. It wasn't real.

"Addison, sweetie, you don't want to go back there," she whispered softly in my ear.

"LET ME GO! I NEED TO SEE HER!" I screamed as loud as I could, finally escaping from her grasp and rushing down the narrow hallway to my parents' bedroom, ignoring the view of my father crying in the living room, slumped against the wall.

I stopped in the doorway as a man in a black suit moved away from the bed and nodded at me.

"She's sleeping. She's just sleeping," I mumbled to myself as I caught my first glimpse of my mother lying on her side under the covers, facing away from me.

The man in the suit walked over to me and placed a gentle hand on my shoulder. "I'm sorry for your loss."

I didn't even look at him; I couldn't take my eyes off of my mom.

As he walked by me and left the room, my feet slowly carried me closer to the bed, closer to where she lay sleeping, just sleeping.

I rounded the end of the bed and finally saw her face—so peaceful and calm.

"Mom?"

There was no reply and I took another step closer to the bed, looking for signs of life, movement, anything—something to tell me that this wasn't happening.

"No, no, no, no, no," I mumbled through my tears as I stood next to the bed just staring down at her, unable to make my feet move.

My chest hurt and my vision is blurred from all of the tears pouring out of my eyes. I wrapped my arms around my waist and continued to chant my denial until I was screaming the words over and over.

"NO. NO. NO. NO. NO. NO!"

"No, no, no, no."

The sound of my own voice pulls me back to the present, and I try to get my brain to catch up with what's happening right now.

"ADDISON!"

Zander's shout makes me jump, and I realize I've been staring at the empty pill bottles thinking about the past instead of doing what I need to do to help Meg.

With shaking hands I dial 9-1-1 and tell the dispatcher with a monotone voice that I think my friend just tried to kill herself.

Zander leaves me alone with Meg to go outside and wait for the ambulance once he's made sure that I'm okay and not going to stand here doing nothing but wish things had been different between her and I. I'm sitting by her side with her head in my lap, trying not to cry as she looks up at me. Her eyes are glazed over with what I now know are sleeping pills that were prescribed by her doctor to help keep the nightmares away.

"Why? Why didn't you tell me?" I whisper to her as I run the palm of my hand down her cheek.

"Silly, Addy, we don't tell each other things," she slurs with a smile. "Everything is just hunky-dory if we don't talk."

I blink back tears as I stare down at her.

"I'm sorry. I'm so sorry."

A laugh bubbles out of her as her hand weakly reaches up and lightly smacks me on the arm.

"You're so silly. It's not your fault. It's MY fault. It's all my fault. Everything is my fault. They died because of me. Me, me, me. All my fault. I'm so sleepy," she mumbles almost incoherently before her eyes drift closed.

"No, Meg, wake up! You can't go to sleep. Please, Meg, open your eyes," I beg as the tears fall down my cheeks.

Her eyes slowly blink back open, but they don't focus on me. She stares blankly at a spot above my head.

"I shouldn't have snuck out to that party. I shouldn't have drank so much. It's my fault you came to get me. It's my fault that truck hit you. My fault, my fault, my fault," she whispers sadly. "I'm going to make it right. It should have been me."

I shake my head frantically back and forth, not really understanding what she's saying but knowing that this isn't right. None of this is right. None of this should be happening right now, and I'm ashamed of myself for not being a good friend and not knowing what she kept bottled up inside of her.

As Meg floats in and out of consciousness, I remember Dr. Thompson's recent words of wisdom and do something I haven't done in a long time.

I pray.

Chapter Thirteen

Don't Speak

"You can't expect the people around you to know what you want from them if you keep everything bottled up inside, Addison," Dr. Thompson informs me as she gets comfortable in her chair across from me and reaches for her coffee cup.

The cup is white and has pink child-like writing on it that says "World's Best Mom." It reminds me of the mug I made for my mom one year for Mother's Day years and years ago. I briefly wonder if it's still in the cupboard with all the other coffee cups at my parents' house but probably not. I'm sure it's long gone, along with the rest of my mom's things.

"Your anger is like a living, breathing thing. It needs to be let out or it's just going to slowly eat away at you. Your father has learned how to communicate with people in rehab; he knows that he's wronged those he loves, and he knows that they are going to be mad at him. You've been skirting around the big issues with him because you're afraid to rock the boat. You're still so worried about him and what he'll do that you aren't focusing on yourself. You aren't going to be able to get past your disappointment with him until you finally admit to him what his drinking did to you. The two of you need to talk about it and move forward."

That's so much easier said than done. My father and I have never had the type of relationship where we sit down and talk about our feelings. That was always something I did with my mother. My dad is a good person to call when you're in a bind or you need help lifting something heavy, and he's always there with a joke or something to say to make you laugh, but he's never done the touchy-feely thing. He's never been a person I felt like I could go to with a problem or to lean on. Doing so now when he's fresh out of rehab, and probably one stressful situation away from going back, doesn't seem like the best idea.

"Don't be afraid to lay it all out for him, Addison. It's time for someone else to take away some of the burdens that trouble you. He's an adult and it's time he takes some responsibility for his actions."

After sitting in the hospital room for two hours, we finally get word from the doctor that Meg is going to be okay. Meg admitted to only taking a few of the sleeping pills once they were able to get her talking in the ambulance. They still pumped her stomach just in case and were able to get away with just bandaging the cuts on her arm without any of them needing stitches. We won't know how long she'll need to stay until she can get a full exam from a psych doctor. For now, she's safe and she's alive and that's all that matters.

"Are you sure you don't want to go back to your place first and get cleaned up?" Zander asks softly as we pull into the bakery parking lot.

I glance down at myself and realize my shirt is dotted with Meg's blood. Zander puts the car in park, and I don't say a word as I stare at the red splotches on my T-shirt and touch each of them with the tip of my finger.

"I shouldn't have left. She's all alone there. She doesn't have anyone but me," I mumble as I continue to trace the bloodstains, thinking about the words she spoke to me about both of them being gone and how it was all her fault. I can only assume she meant her parents, and it breaks my heart all over again that all this time we had so much more in common than I really knew.

Zander reaches over the console and grabs my hand, pulling it up to his lips and kissing the top of it. I look over at him as he takes his other hand and runs it over the top of my head and down the side of my face.

"She's fine, Sugar. They're going to have her heavily sedated until tomorrow."

I nod my head in response to him, but I still feel guilty. I left her alone to deal with her demons, and now I'm leaving her alone in the hospital. It doesn't feel right.

"I have to go into work for an hour to finish up some paperwork. I'll make sure to check on her and let you know what's going on," he promises.

I want to tell him I love him. It hits me like a punch to the face as I sit here staring at him, covered in my friend's blood, the guilt eating me alive. I want to tell him that I'm only able to breathe right now because he's sitting next to me taking care of me.

But I don't. I can't. I won't burden him with my feelings until he knows everything about me. Instead, I lean over toward him and rest my forehead against his and let out a deep sigh.

"Thank you for being here today," I tell him softly.

"Don't thank me for something like that. Of course I'm here, and I'm not going anywhere. You know that, don't you, Addison?"

His voice is filled with worry and concern, and I almost wonder if he knows that I was about to tell him I love him but stopped myself. I wonder if he knows there's more to my story than I've told him so far and this is his way of reassuring me that nothing I say or do can chase him away.

It's wishful thinking on my part. I *want* to believe all of those things, and I *want* them to be true so much that I'm just assuming he can read my mind and know what I'm thinking.

"I should go inside and talk to my dad," I tell him, pulling away from his face and moving to open the car door. All I want to do is pull him close and kiss him, forget about what happened today and forget about the part I played in it, but I can't. I have responsibilities.

"You'll call me if you need me, right?" he asks through the open window as I step out into the parking lot and close the door behind me.

"I will, I promise."

The shop is empty when I walk through the front door, and I'm thankful for that. I probably should have taken Zander's advice and gone home first to shower and change, but for the first time in a long time, I just want to talk to my dad. I want the comfort of his wisdom and the reassurance that only a father can give.

"Whose blood is that? Is that your blood? What the hell happened?" my dad frantically asks me as soon as I walk through the door. He races around the front counter and grabs onto my arms, searching me for injuries.

"I'm fine. It's not my blood," I tell him in a tired voice as he takes my face in his hands and turns it side to side making sure I'm telling the truth.

"What happened? Did that Zander guy do something?"

I pull back and look at him like he's crazy.

"What? No! It's from Meg, but she's fine," I say quickly when his eyes bug out in shock.

"What happened to Meg?"

I clear my throat uncomfortably and turn away from him, mumbling the words quietly. "Today was a really bad day for her. She took some sleeping pills...too many. And she broke a few things around her apartment and cut herself, hence the reason for the blood."

It's quiet behind me for so long that I finally turn around to see if my dad even heard me. He's still standing in the same spot with his hands on his hips and a surprising look of fury on his face. His lips are pinched tightly together and the hands on his hips are balled into fists.

"I knew that girl was trouble. She's done working here, and I don't want you anywhere near her."

"Excuse me?" I fire back at him, gritting my teeth in anger.

"You heard me. That isn't the type of person you need to be associated with, Addison. She's bad news and this just proves it. She tried to kill herself for God's sakes. Someone like that is just..."

My dad cuts off what he's about to say, most likely because of the rage coming off of me in waves. I can feel it boiling inside of me, and I want to scream. I want to shove everything off of the table next to me so it can crash to the floor and some of this anger can be taken out on something other than him. He has no idea how much Meg and I have in common, and I should feel sorry for him because he's so dense when it comes to this subject, but I don't. He doesn't know how Meg and I met, and he doesn't know we have matching scars on our wrists to remind us every single day of our weaknesses. He doesn't know because he was too busy spending another sixty days in rehab forgetting about the daughter he left at home to fend for herself and say good-bye to her mother all on her own.

"Someone like that is just *what*? Go ahead, finish that sentence."

I want to hear him say it. I want to hear him admit that someone like that is poison, damaged, broken, pathetic, weak...all of the words I know are flowing through his head right now, all of the words I've associated with myself over the last year.

"Come on, Dad, tell me what you really think of Meg. How do you *really* feel about someone who tries to kill themselves? What do you think about the kind of person who could be so weak and in so much pain that they feel like there's no other way out, no other way to stop the hurting?"

I don't even realize I'm advancing on him until I'm right in front of him staring up at his six-foot-two frame, waiting for him to tell me all of the things I already know about myself.

"I understand she's your friend and that you're probably upset about what happened—"

"You don't understand shit!" I yell at him. "Do you know what I was doing a year ago next weekend, Dad? I was sitting at Mom's grave, full of pills with a razor blade in my hand, curled up next to her headstone wishing I could be anywhere else but here without her. All of those things you're thinking about Meg right now—how she's a bad person and hopeless and broken and a lost cause—well guess what? So am I."

I shove the sleeve of my shirt up to my elbow and thrust my arm in his face and watch it lose all of its color as he listens to what I'm saying and stares at the long white scar on the inside of my wrist.

"This is what hopeless and broken looks like, Dad. It looks the exact same way as Meg, and it feels the exact same way she feels. It's *feeling* alone and *being* alone and realizing that everyone you loved and depended on left you and didn't give a shit about you enough to be there for you," I shout as he slowly shakes his head back and forth in denial.

"Oh, Addison, no," he cries softly.

I'm sure this isn't exactly what Dr. Thompson had in mind when she advised me to finally talk to my dad, but now that I've started, I can't stop the venom from flying out of my mouth.

"She died and they may as well have just buried you right next to her. You got rid of all of her things, and you refuse to talk about her or acknowledge her. One day she was here and everything was fine, and the next it was like she never even existed. We don't talk about how much we miss her, and we don't talk about the memories we have of her, and God forbid we even say her name. The holidays are spent ignoring all of the traditions we shared with her and shitting all over everything she ever blessed us with because NO ONE WILL TALK ABOUT HER!"

I want to cry. I *should* be crying. It's overwhelming to be telling my father all of the things I've kept to myself the last year, and my emotions are going haywire. Every truth I speak is like a knife to both of our hearts. I know I'm hurting him, I know I'm ripping open old wounds, and the look on his face tells me the wounds are festering and bleeding and excruciating, but I don't care. I *want* him to hurt. I want him to feel a fraction of the pain I've felt and had to deal with on my own all this time.

"This is because of Zander, isn't it? He's filling your head with things and turning you against me," my dad argues, still shaking his head back and forth as I pull my arm away but refuse to cover up my scar. I always wear long-sleeve shirts and always have something covering my arm so no one can see what I've done. I'm finished with that now. I'm finished with the lies and the hiding and the pretending.

"Do you even hear yourself right now? Why would you think Zander had *anything* to do with what I'm feeling or what I've done? You don't even know him."

My dad lets out an irritated laugh and nervously runs his hands through his hair.

"And neither do you. You've been spending a lot of time with him lately. I'm glad you're getting out and away from this place, but I just don't trust that guy," he tells me.

"Oh that's rich coming from you," I fire back.

"What the hell is that supposed to mean?"

I roll my eyes at him and take a step back, putting some distance between us.

"You know exactly what it means. I may not have known him for very long, but I trust him. I've known *you* my whole life and I can't say the same."

The irritation falls from his face, and it's quickly replaced by sadness. I know my words did that to him, but I don't care. We've been tiptoeing around each other since he came home and I'm done. I can't keep worrying that something I say or do will force him back to drinking. Dr. Thompson is right. He's an adult and he makes his own choices. I can't keep being responsible for the bad ones he makes. For the first time I finally understand and believe what she's been telling me all along: it's not my fault.

"Meg's going to be fine by the way," I inform him, bringing the focus back to the important matter at hand, knowing that all of the things I shouted at him about my mom fell on deaf ears, just like always. I turn away from him and stalk to the front door flinging it open and walking outside, ignoring my dad as he calls after me over and over.

Chapter Fourteen
Dear Love

"You're the only one who can make yourself happy again, Addison. You've had the power all this time. You just needed to find a reason to *be* happy again," Dr. Thompson tells me. "If Zander makes you happy, why are you hesitating?"

I don't have an answer for her. I honestly don't know why I'm stopping myself from letting him in all the way, aside from fear that he'll leave. But I know that's not true. He's not the type of person who would do that, and I know it from the bottom of my heart.

"I think you know by now that you can't live your life in fear. You know that each and every moment you have on this earth is precious and should never be taken for granted. Don't waste the time you have being afraid. Get your ass in gear and be happy!"

I sit there and stare at Dr. Thompson in shock for so long that she finally rolls her eyes at me. It's something my mom would have said and done to me, and I'm taken aback.

It's the first time I've ever walked out of Dr. Thompson's office with chills on my arms.

I'm standing on Zander's small front porch, soaking wet, trying to gather up the courage to knock. I had to call a cab when I stormed out of the bakery because Zander picked me up early this morning for our picnic so my car was still parked at my apartment. I didn't feel like waiting in the parking lot for it to arrive and chance my dad seeing me and coming out to talk to me, so I walked until the cab pulled up. I walked seven blocks in the pouring rain, the dark clouds and torrential downpour matching my mood.

But standing here with my hair plastered to my face and my wet clothes clinging to my body, I feel like I'm in a stupid, tragic romance movie where the heroine runs through the rain to get to the man she loves. It's too cliché even for me, but I'm here now, and I might as well knock and get it over with. I need Zander. I need the comfort of his arms and his soothing voice to tell me everything will be okay.

The door flies open before I can even finish knocking once. Zander stands there in his hospital scrubs and it takes me a moment to remember why I'm there. I've never seen him in his scrubs, and it's a sight to behold. They are the same color blue as his eyes, and all I can think about is taking them off of him.

"Oh my God, did you walk all the way here? Why didn't you call me?" he asks in shock as he glances out to his driveway and doesn't see my car. "Hurry up, get in out of the rain."

He pulls me inside and closes the door, immediately wrapping his arms around me and holding me close.

"I'm getting you all wet," I complain as he quickly rubs his hands up and down my back in an attempt to warm me up.

"I don't care about that. Why didn't you call me? You promised you'd call if you needed something. I would have picked you up," he scolds.

I burrow my face into his neck and breathe deep, letting the smell of his soap and cologne fill me and calm my nerves and wash away my anger.

"I'm sorry. I got into a fight with my dad, and I just needed to leave. I just needed to be here with you."

I speak against his throat and can't help but place a small kiss right against his Adam's apple. His hospital scrubs are now completely wet thanks to me, but at least now I can feel the heat from his body and the chill that spreads through my skin has nothing to do with my wet clothes and everything to do with the man holding me.

I pull out of his arms a little so I can stare up at his face. He brings one hand up and pushes some of my wet hair off of my forehead.

"You need to get out of these wet clothes. I'll get you some towels," he tells me softly as he starts to move away, but I clutch onto the front of his wet hospital scrub shirt and pull him back up against me.

"I have a better idea. How about you just take your clothes off too, and we can kill two birds with one stone," I tell him with a smile.

I watch as he wets his lips and swallows nervously before he speaks again. "Don't tempt me right now. It's hard enough as it is trying not to stare at your see-through shirt. I'm trying to be a gentlemen here."

He starts to move away again, and before he can take his eyes off of me, I quickly reach for the hem of my wet shirt and pull it up and off of my body, tossing it to the hardwood floor where it lands with a *splat*. His mouth drops open as he stares at me standing right in front of him in nothing but a white, lace bra and wet jeans.

"What are…oh Jesus…I…holy…wow…"

I can't help but laugh as he stutters through his words while he looks me up and down. I thought I would be more nervous about this, but I should have known better. Everything about Zander makes me feel comfortable, like I can finally be myself.

Reaching for the snap of my jeans, I slide the button through the hole and then slowly lower the zipper.

"I think I might need some help getting these wet jeans off."

When I hook my thumbs into the waist of my jeans, Zander finally finds his voice and quickly rests his hands on top of mine to stop my attempt of removing them on my own.

"Sugar, you're driving me crazy. What are you doing?" he whispers.

"I know I'm a little inexperienced when it comes to this, but I do believe I'm taking my clothes off. You should probably do the same," I tell him with a smile.

"You just had a fight with your dad and you walked halfway here in the pouring rain. I don't want you doing something you'll regret because you're upset."

Grabbing onto his hands at my waist, I pull them up to my face and place his palms on my cheeks, holding them in place.

"You're right. I am upset and I had a bad night, but I would never, ever regret this. Not with you. I'm here because I need you. I'm here because I want you. I'm here because I *love* you."

I can't take the words back, and even though I know I should have waited to tell him, I couldn't do it. I need him to know how I feel. I need him to know that this isn't some spur of the moment decision based on my erratic emotions. I may not have planned on this happening tonight, but the fact that his face and his home and his smile are the only images that popped into my head as soon as I walked out of the bakery mean something. He's important to me, and I need him to know that.

"Say something," I whisper to him as he stands in front of me with his hands on my face and stares into my eyes.

Maybe this is too much for him. Maybe he's not ready for something like this, and I just screwed everything up by telling him I love him. No matter what, I will never regret telling him how I feel. I'm done keeping things bottled up inside of me—the good and the bad.

"Say it again," he replies softly as his thumb brushes back and forth over my cheekbone.

"I love you," I reply without hesitation.

"Oh thank God."

His lips crash to mine, and I smile against his mouth as he wraps his arms around me and pulls me against him. When his tongue brushes against mine, I can't help but whimper. I love kissing this man, I love touching this man, and I don't want to wait any longer.

I don't know if he senses my impatience or it's just a mixture of his own, but Zander quickly lifts me up against him, and I wrap my legs around his waist as he turns and heads down the hall toward his bedroom, never breaking the kiss.

He stumbles with me in the dark hallway, smacking into the wall every few feet as we struggle to remove his wet shirt in between kisses and laughs. When we finally make it into his room, he sets me down on my feet next to the bed, and we help each other remove the rest of our wet clothes. In the darkness of the bedroom, I can just make out his features from the streetlamp shining in through the window. He smiles at me before scooping me back up and then laying me down gently on top of his bed, quickly putting on a condom before covering my body with his own.

He takes some of his weight off of me by leaning up on his elbows, and I wrap my legs around his hips to keep him as close to me as possible.

"Say it one more time," he whispers as he stares down at me.

I chuckle before looking at him in complete seriousness and repeating the words one more time. "I love you, Zander."

He lets out a sigh of contentment and rests his forehead against my own.

"I have loved you from the first moment I saw you."

I want to cry at the sweetness of his words, but now isn't the time for crying. Now isn't the time for being sad. Now is the time to live...and be happy.

"Are you sure about this?"

Butterflies flap wildly in my stomach at his words. Not only does he love me, he *cares* about me. He wants me to be okay, and I know without a doubt that if I changed my mind, none of that would be different.

But I am not about to change my mind. I want him more than I could ever even tell him.

"I am more sure about this than anything in my life."

He closes his eyes and sighs peacefully again, shifting his hips so I can feel him against me and know without a doubt how much *he* wants this and wants me.

Sliding my hands through his hair, I pull his mouth to mine as he positions himself between my legs and slowly begins to push himself inside me.

I wince at the shock of pain, and he pulls away from my lips to whisper apologetic words and professions of love against my mouth. "I'm sorry, I'm sorry, I love you."

He pauses his movements and holds himself steady above me. I lean up and kiss him again, needing the connection of his lips against mine to calm my nerves.

"It's okay. I'm okay," I tell him quietly as I command my body to relax and remind myself that it won't hurt for long. "Please, I'm okay. Keep going."

The pained look and worry on his face about hurting me melts my nerves, and I tighten my legs around his waist and pull him deeper into me until he pushes past the barrier and I can let out the breath I'd been holding.

The burning discomfort quickly eases as we move against each other, and Zander keeps reminding me how much he loves me, over and over. He touches and kisses me everywhere he can reach, and it's not long before the pleasure of being with him like this erases the pain and I can enjoy what is happening. He moves his hand between us, and with feather-light touches, he ignites a fire inside of me that has me clutching tightly onto his hair and throwing my head back on the pillow while he kisses my neck. Nothing has ever felt this amazing; nothing compares to feeling Zander touch me and move inside of me. I never expected my first time to be like this. I never expected to feel anything other than relief to get it out of the way. I never want this to end, and I'm shocked to feel my release slowly creeping up on me as he moves his body and his hand torturously slow against me.

"Zander, Zander..."

I chant his name over and over as my toes curl and pleasure shoots through every inch of my body. I don't even recognize the sounds that are coming out of my mouth as I push my hips frantically against his to prolong everything I'm feeling. He swallows my cries with his lips as he begins moving faster and harder, and I wrap my arms tightly around his shoulders to keep him as close to me as possible. He's strong and solid, warm and gentle, and I want to stay wrapped around him forever.

He tells me he loves me over and over through his own release, and I hold on to him as securely as I can, never wanting to let him go or have this moment end.

Zander finally collapses on top of me, and I smile happily feeling all of his weight and the racing of his heart against my chest. After a few minutes, he rolls off of me, leaning over the side of the bed to dispose of the condom in the trashcan. He quickly slides back next to me and wraps his arms around my waist, turning me to my side and pulling my back against his chest. Reaching down, he pulls the covers up over both of us and then snuggles against me, smothering my cheek, my neck, and my shoulder with tiny kisses until I giggle when he gets to a ticklish spot.

"I love you, Addison," he whispers against my ear before resting his head on the pillow behind me.

Closing my eyes, I slide my fingers through his hand resting on my waist and pull his arm tighter around me, drifting off to sleep faster than I have in a long time.

Chapter Fifteen

I'll Stand by You

"I know you used to be a completely different person, Addison. It's hard to find that person again when so many heavy things keep getting piled on top of your shoulders," Dr. Thompson tells me as she holds her coffee cup close to her mouth and then blows gently on the hot liquid. This week's cup had little blue snowflakes on it with the words "Let it Snow" painted in silver and blue. I glance out the window at the bright sunshine and wonder why she's using a winter mug when it's almost eighty degrees out.

"You had friends and you had fun and you were carefree. Excuse my language, but it's time to shit or get off the pot, as they say," Dr. Thompson tells me with a smile.

I'm momentarily stunned by her choice of phrases. My mom used to say that to me and my father all the time, and even though I'm used to Dr. Thompson's bluntness by now, this one comes out of left field.

"You're doing good and you're forming healthy relationships. Keep that momentum going, Addison. Be a good friend; be the wonderful, thoughtful person you always used to be and that I know you still can be. The more you do it, the easier it will be to get your old self back."

Walking through the hospital halls, I can't help but smile. Even though I'm worried about Meg, and I'm nervous to see her, all I can think about is Zander and our night last night. When I woke up this morning, I was still wrapped in his arms and it was very difficult to force myself to get out of bed. All I wanted to do was stay in bed with him snuggled under the covers and forget about the outside world, but I can't do that right now. When I checked my phone, I had a text from Meg saying she could have visitors and three missed calls from my dad. Right now, I only have the strength to deal with one crisis at a time, so my dad will have to wait.

"Knock, knock," I announce as I stick my head into the open doorway of Meg's room. She's sitting up in bed, flipping through the channels on the television, and gives me a big smile as I enter the room.

"It's about time you got here. The cable channels in this hospital suck ass."

I laugh as I pull the extra chair in the room closer to the bed and take a seat while she powers off the television.

"Sooooo, what's new?" I ask with a smile, taking a page from Zander's book and trying to lighten the situation a little. I want Meg to feel comfortable talking to me. I want her to know that I'm her friend and I'm here for her. It's time to change how I act around people, and I want to start with her.

"Oh, you know, the usual. Just a little depression and suicide attempt to brighten everyone's day," she says with an uncomfortable chuckle.

The silence hangs in the air between us as Meg pulls at the frayed edges of the blanket that covers her legs.

"What happened, Meg?" I ask her softly.

She lets out a huge sigh and leans back against the pillows, her face turning up toward the ceiling as she contemplates her words.

"Two years ago I was in college. I was going to school for elementary education. I still lived at home and commuted back and forth to classes," she explains quietly, her eyes still trained on the ceiling tiles. "One night things got a little out of hand at a party, and I had way too much to drink. My parents always said I could call them any time I got myself into trouble, so I called them to pick me up since all of my friends were just as wasted as I was, if not more. On the way back home, my dad was lecturing me about drinking, and I said something sarcastic. He turned around to look at me, and the next thing I knew, everything around us exploded. He went left of center and we hit a truck head on. They were killed instantly. I walked away with a sprained wrist and a cut on my head. I had two little injuries, and they had their lives taken away. My extended family wanted nothing to do with me after that. I was already the black sheep because I was a little wild, but this just proved to everyone what a bad seed I was. I killed my parents...two years ago yesterday."

Meg finally turns her face toward me, and all I can think about doing is wrapping her in my arms and telling her everything will be okay.

So I do.

Getting up out of my chair, I perch myself on the edge of her hospital bed.

"Move over," I command as I swing my legs up on top of the blankets.

"Are we going to cuddle? Ooooh, can we spoon?" she asks with a laugh as she scoots over on the bed.

"Shhhhh, don't ruin the moment," I tell her as I wrap one arm around her shoulder and pull her next to me. She rests her head on my shoulder and we sit together quietly on her hospital bed for a long time.

"I'm so sorry for what happened to your parents. It's not your fault. And your family are a bunch of jackasses," I say angrily, breaking the silence.

Meg lets out a little laugh and wraps her arm around my waist.

"Can I give you their phone numbers so you can call them and tell *them* that?"

We laugh together, but I hope she knows that I would do exactly that and more for her. I would drive to each of their houses and tell them off if it would make things better for her.

"I'm sorry. I was a jerk to you," I whisper.

"You weren't a jerk. You had your own crap to deal with. And it's not like I offered up this information about myself. You didn't know."

"But I *should* have known. I never used to be such a crappy friend. I used to be the person everyone went to with their problems…" I trail off.

"So what happened? I know your dad kind of sucks. Or at least he used to. He seems pretty cool to me, but I don't know him that well aside from working with him the last few weeks," Meg says with a shrug.

I don't even hesitate to tell her my story. I owe her an explanation so she understands that I used to be a better person and that I'm trying to get that back, little by little.

I tell her about losing my mom, but I don't go into too many details. It doesn't seem right to focus too much on my problems when she's the one in the hospital, but I still want her to understand. She had an inkling about my dad from bits and pieces of conversations she overheard in the last year, but she never wanted to pry so she never came right out and asked.

After I unload on her, Meg and I talk more about her parents, and she promises me that she will talk to me whenever she is feeling guilty or depressed. No more pills, no more drowning in sorrow alone. We are *both* going to be better friends to each other and I feel hopeful that both of our futures look brighter.

Meg asks about Zander, and I can't hide the blush from my cheeks or the smile from my face. She knows just from the look on my face what happened last night and lets out an ear-piercing scream that causes several nurses to come running. After we finish convincing them that everything is fine and burst into a fit of giggles when they leave, I hesitate to ask for advice. Even though I don't want to burden Meg with my problems, she insists that I do. She needs something else to focus on aside from her own problems, and I guess she's right. I realize that sitting here in the hospital, talking to her for over an hour, that even though I'm dredging up old memories and problems and talking about current ones, the feeling of dread that usually pools in my stomach isn't there. I'm comfortable talking to Meg, and it feels very good to have another girl to talk to. I love Zander and I know I can talk to him about anything, but there's just something different about having a girlfriend to confide in.

"I told him I love him," I tell her sheepishly.

"Oh, holy shit, this is serious. More serious than giving up your V-card."

I smack her on the arm and tell her to keep her voice down when a nurse walks by and looks in on us.

"Are we moving too fast? It's too fast, isn't it? I feel like everyone is looking at us like we're crazy. And my dad isn't too fond of him. God knows why," I complain with a roll of my eyes.

"I hate when people say that to someone else. 'Oh my, they got married too soon,' or 'But they haven't even known each other that long.' What business is it of theirs to judge *your* relationship? Only the two of you know what's right or what's wrong. I know for a fact that you wouldn't have had sex with someone if you didn't trust them completely. And I've seen the way he looks at you and the way he takes care of you; his eyes follow you everywhere making sure you're okay. No one can tell you whether you're moving too fast or too slow. You're moving at exactly the right speed for the two of you and that's all that matters."

When Meg finishes up, I stare at her in shock, surprised by her insight.

"How the hell did you get so smart?"

She shrugs and gives me a cocky smile. "It's easy fixing other people's problems. It's my own that can suck it."

We talk for a few more minutes, and when I'm confident that she's going to be okay, I promise to call her later that evening and step out of the room so she can get some rest before she meets with one of her shrinks.

Digging through my purse to try and locate my cell phone to text Zander, I don't pay attention to where I'm going and run right into someone's chest.

"Oh my God, I'm so sorry!" I exclaim, looking up at a blond guy in hospital scrubs with a stethoscope around his neck.

"It's okay. I'm good," he says with an easy smile.

"Addison? Excuse me, Addison Snow?"

I turn when one of Meg's nurses jogs up to me with my cell phone in her hand.

"You left this in Meg's room. She told me to try and catch you before you left," she says, handing the phone over.

I thank her and she quickly walks away to go back to work.

"You're name is Addison Snow? I thought you looked familiar."

I look back at the guy I ran into, surprised that he's still standing next to me.

"I'm sorry, do I know you?"

He reaches up with both of his hands and fiddles with the stethoscope around his neck. "You probably don't remember me. You were pretty out of it the last time I saw you. You look good though. I'm glad you're doing so well. Zander said you were doing alright, but it's nice to see it first-hand."

I stare at him in confusion, not really sure what he's talking about or when he would have seen me last. But since he knows Zander, I'm assuming he must be a friend of his or one of his co-workers. I can't help but smile knowing that he talks about me to his friends.

"Do you work with Zander or something?"

He shakes his head at me, continuing to tug the ends of his stethoscope back and forth around his neck. "No, he works down in Radiology, but we met in college. I'm an intern in the Emergency Room, which is how I met you."

Bits and pieces of broken memories from my time in the emergency room flutter through my mind and a chill crawls up my spine.

"I need a liter of O negative in here immediately. She's losing a lot of blood."

"Can you tell me your name? Keep your eyes open for me."

"Someone get me a pressure cuff and call the OR."

"Her name is Addison. Addison Snow and she's eighteen years old."

"Hey there, Sugar, open your eyes. Come on, open your eyes and look at me."

"BP is seventy over forty-five. I need that blood NOW!"

"Addison, hey, it's okay. Shhhh, you're okay. I'm right here, Addison."

"Man, Zander was out of control that day when you were brought in." The guy's voice breaks through my memories, and

I find it harder and harder to breathe while he continues on. "I've known him for a lot of years, but I've never seen him that devastated or freaked out as he was when he stopped by to talk to me and they wheeled you in. We tried to get him to leave while we worked on you, but that guy was determined. Something about making a promise to your mom...I don't know. He was the only one able to get you talking, though, so we kind of had to let him stay."

I don't say one word to him in response to his story and his trip down memory lane. I can't speak, I can't breathe, and everything around me looks blurry, and I realize I turned away from him and began running down the halls of the hospital with tears falling down my cheeks.

He shouts my name as I run towards the elevator, but I don't turn around or answer him. The only thought going through my mind is that it was all a lie. Everything between us, every moment, every touch, every word...it was all a lie.

Chapter Sixteen

Don't Follow

"People in your life will let you down sometimes. It's a fact of life, Addison. What matters is how you handle it," Dr. Thompson explains.

The smell of hazelnut permeates the room as I watch Dr. Thompson lift her coffee cup to her mouth and take a sip. I used to love the smell of hazelnut. My mom would buy fresh hazelnut coffee beans and grind them herself every morning.

"Obviously, I don't know how to handle it. I'm so used to people letting me down that I've become immune to it at this point. I expect it, it happens, and then I just move on and never want anything more to do with them."

Dr. Thompson sets down her cup and folds her hands in her lap.

"No one is perfect. People make mistakes. Just because they hurt you doesn't mean they don't still love you or care for you. There are lots of different reasons for someone to make the choices they have in life. If you don't allow them to get close to you again or try to make amends, you'll constantly find yourself alone. I don't want you to be alone, Addison. You deserve to be surrounded by people who love you and have your best interests at heart. You used to always be able to see the good in people. I want you to be able to get back to that point again. I want to see you happy again. I don't feel like my work is done here until you can finally be happy again."

Dr. Thompson didn't know me before—back when I was surrounded by people who loved me and I didn't have a care in the world except for being young and having fun. She's right though; I always saw the good in people first. Even if they disappointed me in some way, I was still able to find redeeming qualities in them and still wanted to be close to them. I forgave easily, I forgot quickly, and nothing left permanent scars on my heart. I want to get that person back. I feel like she's just beyond my reach. I feel like I'm teetering on the edge of being stuck in sadness and depression or moving forward with life and allowing myself to be happy. One good, strong gust of wind could push me in either direction. Right now, it feels like my future happiness all depends on which way the wind is blowing.

I don't knock on the door to Zander's house when I get there. He had showed me where the spare key was a few weeks ago, so I lift up the welcome mat and pick it up off of the porch floor, sliding it into the lock and opening the door.

It's strange being in his home without him here. Even though he's at work, his presence is everywhere. No matter which way I turn, no matter what room I walk through, I can see him, feel him, hear him…he's everywhere, and for the first time since I met him, it makes me angry. I don't want him invading my life anymore. I don't want to see him everywhere I look or think about memories of the two of us together in every part of the house I walk through. It takes everything in me not to shove all of his mail off of his kitchen table, knock the framed pictures of his family off the walls, or pick up his lamps and throw them against the wall. I want to break him like he broke me. But the things in this house are just that: things. Breaking them won't hurt him; they won't shatter his heart or his soul. These things can be replaced after they've been broken. You only get one heart and soul and what the hell are you supposed to do with those things after they've been destroyed?

I ignore the happy memories of us curled up together on his couch watching a movie and think about the bad things instead. I think about his deception and his lies. I think about how in just seven short weeks I felt so comfortable with him and how it felt like I had met him before. I think about how afraid I was to tell him what I'd done at the cemetery a year ago and how I didn't want him to look at me any differently. It's such a joke, all of the anxiety I had about something that he already knew about. He knew everything about me and never said a word.

I walk into his room and refuse to look at the bed. I refuse to remember how it felt to be wrapped up in his arms and close to his body. I won't let myself think about the words of love he whispered to me and how they were all a lie.

I don't even know what I'm doing in his room. I don't know what I'm looking for or what I hope to find, but I have to do something. I need answers and I need them now. I begin dragging all of the clothes out of his dresser drawers, tossing them onto the floor in huge piles. When each drawer is empty and I find nothing, I move on to his closet, then under his bed, and then to each of his nightstands. I empty the contents of his entire room onto the floor, and when I find nothing that connects him to me or my mother, I crumble to the ground in the middle of clothes, shoes, sports equipment, old textbooks, and photo albums. I've obviously seen too many movies. I've read too many stories where a creepy stranger fills their room with secret photos and notes that implicate them in their deception. Did I really expect to find a box full of black and white photos of me taken with a telephoto lens? I hug my knees to my chest, rocking slowly back and forth.

I don't know how long I sit among his things, staring off into space, but it's not long before I hear his voice behind me.

"If you wanted to do a little housekeeping, I've got some dirty clothes in the laundry room you could have tackled," Zander says from the doorway of his room with an uncomfortable chuckle.

I don't turn around to face him, and I don't move from my spot on the floor. I can tell by his laugh that he knows why I'm here. His friend at work probably told him what happened. It makes me sick to my stomach to know that a stranger knew more about my life than I did and that Zander confided in him instead of me.

"How?"

I only say one word to him, but that one word is enough. He knows exactly what I'm asking for, and he can probably tell by the state of his room that if he doesn't tell me the truth once and for all, this won't be the only damage I do to his home. I've never been filled with this much anger or hurt. I should be ashamed of acting like a child and making a mess, but I'm not.

"I was her radiology tech when she was first diagnosed. I'm the one who ran the initial test on her confirming Leukemia. And then over the two years she was sick, it just happened that I was always the tech on duty when she came in for scans. I started picking her up from her room and taking her down for her scans on my own instead of letting an orderly do it. We had a lot of time to talk."

I close my eyes and think about all the times over those years that my mother needed an MRI or an X-ray or some other imaging test, and it occurs to me that she would have had a lot of time to talk to him, a lot of time to talk about her life and her one and only daughter.

"Did she tell you to stalk me after she was gone or was that something you decided all on your own?" I ask angrily, pushing myself up from the floor so I can face him. I want to see his face. I want to watch and find out if this time, now that I know everything, I can easily recognize the lies.

"I didn't stalk you, Addison. I kept an eye on you to make sure you were okay."

I let out an unattractive snort and roll my eyes at him.

"Oh, I'm sorry, is that the new technical terminology for following someone around, knowing everything about them, and then tricking them into loving you? My bad," I tell him sarcastically.

He closes the distance between us and reaches out for me, but I quickly sidestep him. I don't want his hands on me. I don't want him anywhere near me. His face falls when I continue walking backward until I bump into the wall next to the door.

"I'm sorry, Addison, I'm so sorry. I was going to tell you. I swear to God it was killing me to keep this from you. I knew if I told you too soon that you would walk away. I didn't want to lose you. I love you. Please, you have to believe me when I say that," he begs.

"You don't love me. It was all a lie. You knew everything about me the entire time. This entire time I thought it was real but it never was. You just felt sorry for me," I tell him with a sob.

I don't want to cry in front of him. I don't want to tell him that just being here in the same room with him is cutting holes in my heart that is only being held together by the tiniest of threads.

"It was *never* a lie and I *never* felt sorry for you. I worried about you, and I wanted you to be happy. From the first moment I saw you in that hospital when you were visiting her, I knew I wanted to know you better. It was wrong and I *knew* it was wrong, but I couldn't help it. You were so beautiful and so strong. Every time she got bad news you held it together for her. I've seen grown men break down in front of their families and an entire staff of doctors, but you just held your head high and gave your mom the strength and the courage to keep on fighting," he tells me, reminding me of all the times I just wanted to race out of her hospital room and scream and cry at the unfairness of it all, but I never did. I never wanted her to see how petrified I was of losing her.

"She talked about you constantly. About how close the two of you were and how it scared her to death having to think about what it would do to you when she was gone. She knew your father wouldn't be able to be strong for you, and she worried about how that would affect you. She saw the way I looked at you when I would see you from a distance, and she joked with me about all of the questions I would constantly ask her about you. During her last appointment, she made me promise to find you and make sure you were okay if something ever happened to her."

His words do nothing to ease the betrayal. If anything it makes me feel even more alone and more angry to know just how close he thought he was to my mother that he could make her a promise like that.

I cross my arms over my chest and don't say a word as he continues with his explanation.

"I tried to stay away from you, I swear. I knew it would be crossing so many lines if I tried to contact you after I found out she passed away, so I did my best to ignore the promise I made to her and forget about you and move on," he continues. "But then, one night, I was on my lunch break, and I went upstairs to the ER to talk with my friend Nate. I had just started talking to him about some plans for the weekend when the paramedics burst through the bay doors and we were suddenly surrounded by doctors and nurses and people shouting orders. I took one look at the gurney and my heart instantly fell. I saw you lying there unconscious, your arms, clothes, and the bed covered in blood, and it scared the hell out of me."

I don't want to relive that day again, but I can't help it. Everything is so vivid that I can almost taste the clean, antiseptic smell of the hospital, feel myself being lifted off of the gurney, and hear the shouts and orders of the doctors all around me. Except this time I hear Zander's voice, clear as a bell, asking me to open my eyes and telling me everything will be okay. I hear his voice talking to me right now, and I hear his voice that day in the hospital. Knowing he was the one speaking to me trying to keep me alive should fill my heart with warmth, but it doesn't. I'm embarrassed and I'm ashamed, and I'm angry that he saw me that way. He saw me during one of my weakest moments, and he witnessed just how broken I really am.

"It was my fault. I should have kept my promise to her. It never would have happened if I would have just kept my promise," he states sadly.

"Well, lucky for you, you won't have to be plagued by all of this self-doubt and guilt anymore. You took one look at me and thought you could fix me. I don't need your help, and I don't need your pity," I tell him as I turn away from him and ignore the pain written all over his face. "From now on, stay the hell away from me."

I turn to leave, furious that he basically just admitted he was with me out of guilt. He felt like my suicide attempt was *his* fault for not doing as my mother asked. All this time I thought he was with me because he wanted to be, not because he felt like he had to be.

"Please, Addison, don't leave. Not like this," Zander begs, following behind me as I stalk through his house to the front door.

As I turn the knob and pull open the door, he reaches his arm around me and smacks his palm against the door slamming it closed.

"Please, don't walk away. I'm not explaining this right. I never pitied you, I swear to God. I love you. I've loved you from the first moment I saw you. I don't want to lose you like this."

He's pressed up against my back and his lips are at my ear as he pleads with me. It's so hard to stay strong and not give in when he's standing this close to me. His hand still rests against the closed door and his arm cages me in. I don't know what to do, and I don't know what to believe. I want to turn around and face him so he can wrap his arms around me and take away all of the hurt. But he's the one who caused the hurt this time, and forgetting that fact won't make the pain disappear. I can't keep sweeping my problems under a rug and forgetting about them. Right now, Zander's lies are a huge problem, and I refuse to ignore them.

"You should have been honest with me. I've spent the last year and a half having my father look me in the eye and lie right to my face, over and over. I thought you were different. I thought I could trust you," I tell him as I turn the knob on the door again and open it wide.

His hand falls from around me, and he doesn't try to stop me this time.

"You can trust me, Addison. Please, just tell me what to do and I'll do it. I'll do anything to make this better."

I pause in the doorway and ignore every instinct telling me to turn around and give him another chance. I ignore my heart as it beats furiously in my chest at the thought of walking away and never seeing him again. I've trusted my heart for far too long, and it's done nothing but bring me pain. I need to stop thinking with my heart and use my head instead. If I would have gone into this thinking clearly, maybe I would have seen the signs of his betrayal. I'm done with people taking advantage of me and walking all over my blind trust in them.

"Just stay away from me."

With one last slice to my heart, I walk out of Zander's house and out of his life without saying another word.

Chapter Seventeen

The Last Time

"Life is hard, Addison. Everyone gets knocked down once in a while. The important thing is that you pick yourself back up again. You pick up, you move on, and you do your best. That's all I want is to just see you do your best," Dr. Thompson tells me. "It breaks my heart to see you like this when I know you have so much more life in you and so much more to give people."

I briefly wonder if Dr. Thompson cares about all of her patients as much as she seems to with me. I also wonder if she even *has* any other patients. I know from the shows I've seen on television that people enter and exit through different doors so they never run into each other. Dr. Thompson only has one door so that's not the case in this instance. And obviously life isn't one big happy television show where problems are solved in thirty minutes or less, so she probably just schedules everyone far enough apart so they won't meet awkwardly in the stairwell.

"You just need to learn how to get back up when you fall. Sometimes it's not easy, and most times you just want to stay down so you don't have as far to go the next time it happens, but you can't do that. I won't let you do that. Every time you think of giving up, I want you to think of your mother. I know it hurts, and I know you've tried to stop yourself from remembering her, but I need you to do it. Think about how she would feel if she saw you falling apart. Think about what it would do to her if she knew just how much her death had broken you and changed you."

I nod at Dr. Thompson in agreement, but I don't tell her just how often I do exactly that. I don't confide in her that sometimes, I just want to continue falling apart, keep on hurting myself even more because then maybe she'll come back. I know it's impossible, but it doesn't stop me from hoping that if I disappoint her enough, maybe she'll find a way to speak to me. Maybe I'll get one more chance to hear her voice, even if it is just to tell me to suck it up and stop feeling so sorry for myself.

After the fifth unanswered call in a row from my father as I drive aimlessly through town, I decide to finally go talk to him. It's not like this day can get any worse. Maybe hearing what he has to say will bring me out of the fog I'm in. Nothing makes sense right now, and I feel betrayed by everyone and everything.

"Oh, Addison, thank God. Honey, I'm so sorry. About everything. I don't want to fight with you," my dad exclaims as

I walk through the front door of my parents' home, and he pulls me into his arms.

As angry as I am about my father for all of the things he's done, it all melts away when he hugs me. It's so easy to forget all of the bad things when something feels so right. Being wrapped in his arms makes me feel like a little girl again, back when everything was easy and the only tears I shed were over a scraped knee. I want him to be that person again. I want so badly for him to be the man I always looked up to. I want him to take care of me again for once, and I want him to be my strength and my rock. I'm lost and I'm floundering around, and I need an anchor to keep me in place. As I burrow into his chest and breathe in the scent of his cologne, there's another cloying smell that I would recognize anywhere, and the blood in my veins freezes when it hits my nose. I squeeze my eyes closed and enjoy the last few seconds of warmth before I push out of his arms and back away. I try to keep the feelings of being safe and protected with me, knowing I need them now more than ever, as I take a few steps away from him.

"You've been drinking," I say with a straight face, not allowing my emotions to show, not letting him see how much it hurts to say those words out loud again.

He waves his hand at me and brushes off my statement, moving on quickly to another subject, and I know I already have my answer.

"I've been trying to call you since yesterday. I know you really like that Zander guy, and I'm sorry for being on your case about him, but I finally remembered where I knew him from. I knew he looked familiar and it finally came to me this morning when—"

"Stop. Just stop," I interrupt him with a tired sigh. "I don't want to talk about Zander. I don't want to talk about anything right now but the fact that I can smell it on you."

He runs his hand through his hair nervously, and I know that he's trying to come up with an excuse or some kind of valid explanation for why he "slipped" again. You don't just *slip* when you're an alcoholic and decide to drink again after being sober. The bottle doesn't just *fall* into your hand and you accidentally take a drink. You make a conscious decision to unscrew the lid, tip the bottle back, and take that first sip. You know exactly what you're doing when you swallow the liquid down and continue to pour yourself another glass. It may pool in your belly like sour milk, and you may regret each and every drink you take because you know it's a bad decision, but you still continue to do it.

"What, no excuses? No half-assed explanations as to why you broke your promise again?" I ask him angrily.

"Addison, honey, you have to understand, it's hard. It's not something I can control. It's a disease," he explains.

"No, it's not. MY MOTHER had a disease," I shout at him, unable to keep my temper in check. "She had an infection attacking the blood that ran through her body. She spent years in the hospital and let them pump poisons into her veins week after week. She lost her hair, she threw up, she was always tired, but she kept on fighting until her body finally gave up. SHE had a disease. The only sickness you have is selfishness."

I can't even stand to look at my father right now. Everything about him disgusts me. I don't understand how he turned into such a weak person, but then again it must run in the family since I feel so pathetic right now I could collapse to the floor and never care about getting back up again.

"I know you're angry with me. I'm angry with myself. It's just been so hard, Addison. I keep trying and nothing seems to work. And then this morning I remembered that I had seen Zander at the hospital when your mom was in there, and I just couldn't take the pain of remembering anymore. I'm sorry. I know I've let you down. It won't happen again, I promise."

I watch my father rub the back of his neck nervously, and I want to feel sorry for him, but I can't. I know he's sad and I know he's hurting. I know he misses her and doesn't know what else to do to ease the pain, just like I didn't know what else to do a year ago at the cemetery. I know all of this and yet I know there's nothing I can do for him anymore. I've tried to support him, I've tried to give him tough love, I've kept him close, and I've pushed him away. I've done everything I can to make him want to be healthy, and none of it has worked. I've spent all this time worrying about him that I've lost sight of worrying about myself. I've forgotten how to keep myself healthy and maybe that's why I went into my first real relationship with my eyes closed. I refused to see what was right in front of my face, and now my heart is broken.

"It's not like you've been perfect either. For Christ's sake you tried to kill yourself, Addison. You tried to kill yourself, and I didn't even know about it. I'm your *father* and you didn't even tell me," my dad says angrily, once again turning everything around on me and trying to make me feel guilty. I've been down this path with him so many times that I could probably have spoken these words out loud in unison with him.

"And what would you have done if you *had* known? Left rehab early again? Drank yourself to death this time?" I fire back at him.

"Don't take that tone with me, young lady. I am still your father, and I deserve respect."

I don't laugh in his face, even though I want to. What exactly does he think he deserves respect for? Leaving me when I needed him the most? Doing so much damage to his liver and pancreas that I'm surprised he can even still function and live a normal life?

"I come back here and I want to spend time with you and make all of this up to you, but you won't let me. You don't need me. You're little Miss Independent now and you don't need anyone," he tells me angrily.

"Do you think I *want* to be like this? Do you think I want to take care of everything on my own? I'm so independent because I *had* to be. I don't need you most of the time because I've had to learn how to do this by myself. You weren't there. You were *never* there," I argue.

"This has been hard on both of us, and I'm doing the best I can. You just have to be patient and give me a chance to get through this. I'm going to do better, I promise," he tells me, his voice turning softer and his mood doing a complete one-eighty just like it always does when he's been drinking.

"I'm done, Dad," I finally tell him solemnly as I turn and walk towards the door, knowing that it will probably be the last time I ever set foot in this house again.

"It will be okay, Addison, don't worry. I promise this was the last time," he says to my back as I open the front door and stare out into the front yard where I used to play freeze tag and climb trees with my friends.

"You're right. It *was* the last time. I'm done. I don't need someone in my life that can't be there for me when I need them. We both made a lot of mistakes when she died. We both made choices that weren't healthy for us, but the difference is I was the child and you were the adult. Now the roles are reversed, and I just don't want to do it anymore."

I walk out the door and let it close quietly behind me.

I run up the couple of flights of stairs to Dr. Thompson's office and go right to her door and knock. In my year of coming here, I've never checked in at the front office. At my very first appointment she met me in the hall and told me I could just come right in each week instead of wasting time in the waiting room.

When my knock goes unanswered, I pound on the door again and call her name. I don't have an appointment, but I still had hope that she would be here for an impromptu visit since she always told me I could stop in whenever I needed to. Right now, I need to talk to someone and she is the first person I thought of.

I press my ear to the door to see if I can hear voices on the other side and when I'm met with nothing but silence, I decide to try the handle. As I slowly open the door, the view on the other side forces my heart to beat out of my chest, and my hands start to shake. I creep into the empty room and stand in the middle, turning around slowly in circles and wondering if this is it, if I've finally and completely lost my mind. I need her advice now more than ever. I need her no-nonsense, no bullshit, "this is how it is" words of wisdom. I need to talk to someone who really understands me and can tell me what the hell I should do.

I don't understand what is going on or why she would leave me like this. It doesn't make any sense that some of what I'm feeling right now reminds me so much of how I felt when I lost my mother. She wasn't my mother, but I still feel the pain of that loss all over again as I stand in the room I spent so many hours in, week after week, and see everything gone. No white leather couch, no light blue recliner, no desk, no blinds over the windows that need to be closed to block out the sun, no Thomas Kincaid painting on the wall, no coffee mugs—nothing but an empty room and empty walls. No sign of anyone ever being here.

I can't do this on my own. I'm not strong enough to do this without her. I can't lose another person in my life without any warning. As I struggle to breathe in the middle of the vacant room, a napkin taped to the wall by the door catches my eye, and I drag my feet over to it and rip it down, tears blurring my vision as I read the words she left behind for me.

Chapter Eighteen
Beam Me Up

"Do you remember the day I was released from the hospital and we looked over that list of therapist names?" I ask Meg on my cell phone as I sit in my car staring out the front windshield at the array of headstones and fake flower arrangements.

I didn't even bother trying to make sense of things when I left Dr. Thompson's office the other night. I was exhausted and emotionally drained, and I just wanted to sleep. Unfortunately, sleep wouldn't come. I've tossed and turned the last few nights thinking about my faith in God, my faith in people, and how something so completely impossible might actually be happening to me. I thought about Zander and everything he told me, and against my better judgment, I missed him. It took everything in me not to pick up my cell phone and call him just to hear his voice. He would know what to do, and he would know what to say to make all of this okay, but I couldn't call him. I had no idea how to forgive him for something like this.

Turning my engine off, I pocket my keys and unbuckle my seatbelt, but I don't move to open the door. I haven't been back to this place in a year. A year ago today. It's probably not healthy for me to be here right now, today of all days, but I don't know where else to go.

"Yeah, I think so," Meg replies through the line as I watch a man pull weeds around a headstone a hundred yards away from where I'm parked. "I remember telling you to stay far away from Chronic Halitosis Man. You didn't go to him did you? I warned you about him."

The napkin note I found taped to the wall of the office last night sits in my center console right next to the gearshift. I don't need to read the words again. I already have them memorized, and they repeat on a loop, over and over in my head.

"No, I didn't go to him. I went to that woman you suggested. The one you said you really liked," I tell her, hoping she'll confirm that I'm not crazy.

"Oh awesome! I just spoke to her last night. I have an appointment with her tomorrow as soon as I get released."

I let out the breath I was holding, feeling a little bit less crazy than I did the other night. Maybe she just moved offices or something. That would make much more sense than the ideas I actually have floating around in my brain about spirits and people talking from beyond the grave.

"So did she move? Get a new office or something?" I ask, glancing down at the napkin again.

"No, I don't think so. My appointment is at the same address where I met with her a few years ago," Meg replies.

"On East Avenue, right? On the second floor?"

I hear Meg talking to a nurse in her room, and I wait impatiently for her to finish, tapping my fingers against the steering wheel.

"Sorry, they had to take my blood pressure," Meg tells me, coming back on the line. "Did you say East Avenue? Dr. Thomas isn't on East Avenue. She's on Clifton at the corner of Butternut, and she's on the first floor."

My blood runs cold as I pick up the note and stare at the handwriting.

"You mean Dr. *Thompson*?" I ask, stressing the difference in the name.

"No, Dr. *Thomas*," Meg replies. "No *P*. Who the hell have you been talking to for the last year?"

I don't have an answer for her because I'd like to know the exact same thing. I quickly end the conversation with her, telling her I'll call her later and shove my phone into my pocket. My whole body is filled with dread as I open my car door and slowly climb out. It takes everything in me to force my feet to move off of the blacktop and onto the grass, making my way to her grave. Memories of my last time here flutter in and out of my head, and I try to block them out as I walk up the small incline and pass other headstones of people I don't know. My eyes stay focused on the one I'm heading toward, and it's not long before the sights and sounds around me disappear. I see nothing but the flat cement marker with her smiling face on it, nothing but her name, date of birth, and date of death, nothing but the ground below it that is no longer covered with disturbed earth but freshly mowed grass after a year of upkeep from the groundskeepers.

I don't hear the birds chirping or the tree branches swaying in the breeze. I don't hear the sounds of traffic on the outskirts of the cemetery as people race to get to work or school or wherever else they need to be. I hear nothing but the words I spoke as I sat in the very spot I now stand with nothing but death and ending the pain on my mind.

"I don't know how to live."
"I don't know how to be here without you."

All of the feelings of emptiness and desolation come rushing back. Everything I've tried to keep locked away so I can breathe and function without her surround me, and I clutch my arms around my waist to try and keep it all in. I don't want to let it out. I don't want to feel like I did a year ago. I was in a black hole of depression and nothing could force me out. I close my eyes to ward off the memories, but it doesn't work. I remember birthdays, holidays, vacations, and every conversation we ever had, good or bad. It all comes at me like fireworks bursting right before my eyes. I remember it all, but I don't remember *her*. In my memories her face is fuzzy, and I can't hear her voice. I'm forgetting what she looks like, and I'm forgetting what she sounds like, all because I chose to push it all away and keep it buried where it can't hurt me. I hear her voice in my head telling me to watch my language when I would get fired up about something or complaining to me about how my dad just wanted to watch television instead of going out to dinner. I hear it, but it's not her. It's not her voice echoing in my head; it's Dr. Thompson's. I just want to hear *her* voice again. I want to hear it so badly that I wonder if any of the past year has been real. Dr. Thompson or Thomas or whoever the hell she was reminded me of her. She had the same color hair, the same mannerisms, and the same addiction to hazelnut coffee, but it wasn't *her*. It couldn't have been *her*. It's not possible and it doesn't make sense.

I stare at the headstone and realize it's the only one within my line of vision that doesn't have any flowers on it. It's the only one that shows no sign of anyone having visited it or having carefully picked out just the right decorations to show that this person was missed and someone was thinking about them. I feel guilty that I haven't been back here. I feel ashamed that I haven't let her know how much I've missed her. She should have a hundred different flower bouquets and notes littering her grave. She should have silk flowers and real flowers, flower pots and flower baskets. She was worth more than this barren four-foot by seven-foot plot of land with nothing to show how amazing she was but a patch of sod.

Slowly lowering myself to the ground, I sit in the exact same spot I did a year ago where I let the blood pour out of my veins and into the earth. With the index finger of my right hand, I trace the white scar on the inside of my left wrist as I stare at her picture.

I used to come here all the time after she died. I would come here and talk to her, and every time the wind blew or a bird flew by, I used to imagine it was her trying to answer me. After I got out of the hospital, I looked back on those times when I asked her a question and a windsock hanging from a nearby tree would blow in the breeze, and I called myself all kinds of stupid. The dead don't speak. They don't force a bird to fly by to give you a sign when you're thinking about whether or not killing yourself is a good idea. They don't make the musical notes of a wind chime ring out when you ask if she can hear you.

I pull the crumpled up napkin out of my pocket and stare at it yet again. I trace the cursive handwriting that looks so familiar instead of the scar on my wrist.

"This isn't real. None of this is real," I whisper to the headstone. "I've wanted it too much and my mind is playing tricks on me."

I hold my breath and look around for a leaf to flutter by or a bird to land on the next plot over. Rolling my eyes at my idiocy,

I wad the napkin back up in my hand and throw it angrily into the grass.

My mother always believed in spirits. She believed in the afterlife and she believed people would watch over you after they were gone and they'd find a way to communicate. I always scoffed at her when we would discuss it, but she was adamant.

"Don't laugh. Your grandmother is watching over me. Sometimes I can just feel it," she said to me as we sat at the kitchen table eating dinner while my dad was at work.

"Mom, that's just creepy. Do you really think Grandma is like standing over you watching you make cookies or something? Or going to the bathroom? Oh my God, what if she's watching you and Dad when you...you know..." I asked, trailing off with a laugh.

She picked up the kitchen towel that sat on the table next to her plate and whipped it at me, laughing when it hit me square in the face.

"Well then, she'd definitely get an eyeful since you're father and I...you know...all the time. We're like rabbits," she told me with a wink.

"Oh, eeeeew! La-la-la-la-la-la, I'M NOT LISTENING!" I shouted with my fingers in my ears so I didn't have to hear her.

She reached over and tugged on one of my hands so I would pull a finger out of my ear.

"Seriously, though, you don't believe that your loved ones would want to watch over you after they're gone? Make sure you're okay? Just because they're gone doesn't mean they've forgotten about you. I think it's sad to think of a being in heaven and NOT be with the ones you love," she told me wistfully.

"Well, I think it's weird. There are entirely too many things that my loved ones do NOT need to see me doing," I informed her as I took a bite of my spaghetti.

"Just wait. When you're older and wiser like me. You'll change your mind."

I never did change my mind, though. If anything, after she died, thoughts of my loved ones watching over me made me angry. The bible says Heaven is a place filled with unimaginable beauty. It's a place of joy where there are no tears or sounds of crying. If Heaven really exists, and my mother is there, why in the hell would she ever want to look over her loved ones? There's no joy that can come of that. We're sad and we're depressed and we miss her so much we don't know how to go on living. Why would she *want* to see us like that? Why would she want to step out of the supposed beauty of Heaven and come back to this hell on earth? The answer: she wouldn't. She wouldn't want to watch over me and see me like this. There would be no everlasting happiness for her if she saw what her death has done to my father and me. She would be miserable and her heart would break if she had to be a spirit, fluttering around us day in and day out, seeing how damaged we've become without her.

"I know this isn't real. I wish it was, but it's not. I've wanted to talk to you so badly, so many times…"

I trail off and stare at her picture, trying not to cry. After a few minutes, I push myself up off of the ground and take one last look at her headstone.

"Happy Mother's Day, Mom. I miss you."

I know she isn't really watching over me and she doesn't hear the words I say, but maybe, somehow, she knows. Wherever she is right now, I hope she knows, but probably not.

I turn away and stare angrily at the crumpled up napkin in the grass, refusing to take it with me. It's not real. It was probably just someone playing a trick on me, sticking the knife in a little deeper and twisting the handle. It can't be real.

Walking past the napkin, I head toward my car without a second look back. Coming here was a bad idea, especially today. I thought it would give me answers to the questions plaguing me, but all it did was raise more. I know I can call Meg and she will talk me through this, but my fingers hesitate over the numbers on my cell phone as I unlock my car and get inside.

Slumping back against the seat, I scroll through the contacts in my phone until I get to the z's. A lump forms in my throat when I see his name. More than anything I wish he were here right now, sitting next me in the car, telling me I'm not going crazy and wrapping me in his arms. I should call Meg and let her be my friend. She would say something to make me laugh, and she would know exactly what I should do. The only problem was she never knew my mother. No matter how much I try to explain to Meg what she meant to me, Meg will never fully understand. She never saw us together, she never spent hour after hour with her, week after week, forming a bond with her and making her promises, and she never cared for her or mourned for her or felt an ounce of worry that the promises she made might someday be broken.

I close my eyes and lean my head against the back of the seat, and a small sob escapes my throat.

I pushed him away. He just wanted to protect me, and I pushed him away.

Thinking about all of the time we spent together, each memory fractures my heart into even more pieces because he's not here right now. He lied to me, but I lied to him as well. I was never fully honest with him, and he knew that. He knew that I'd been keeping part of myself hidden from him. Why would he want to confide in me when I couldn't do the same with him?

I need him. I need to know that he was real. I need to feel his hands on my face telling me he loves me. I need to stop keeping everything locked in a vault and just let it all go. I want to break down right now; I want to rage and scream and cry, just like I did a year and a half ago, just like I've wanted to do every day since then, but instead kept it bottled up. I need to grieve. I need to cry for her and remember her, and I need to stop thinking that if I just pretend like she wasn't real and never talk about her with anyone, that it would hurt less. It doesn't hurt less. It hurts more. It hurts so much that I actually contemplated the idea of my mother "speaking" to me through Dr. Thompson and thought it was possible.

I want to pick up my phone and call him, but I can't. Not right now. Not until I can find a way to get through this on my own. He deserves a woman who is whole, not someone struggling to stay sane.

Chapter Nineteen
Can't Cry Hard Enough

I can see her a few feet in front of me. Her short, blonde hair is blowing in the wind and her back is to me. I smile when I see her walking along the beach and race to catch up with her.

"Mom!"

My shout for her goes unanswered, but she probably didn't hear me. The waves crash roughly against the shore, and the wind picks up, whipping my own hair around my face so I have to keep pushing it out of my eyes as I run.

I yell for her again and push my legs to carry me faster so I can reach her before she gets to the mountain of large rocks that jut out from the beach and into the water. She can't climb over those before I get to her. If she does, I'll never get a chance to talk to her.

She continues to walk at a steady pace, not turning her head to look back at me no matter how many times or how loudly I yell.

I'm running as fast as I can now; my chest hurts from breathing heavy as I run, and the muscles in my legs are starting to burn, but it doesn't matter. I need to make it to her. I need to push just a little harder and I'll be there with her. If I can just make it to her, I can tap her on the shoulder and she'll finally turn around. I'll finally see her face and her smile.

I've missed her smile so much.

No matter how hard or long I run, the distance between us continues to grow. She's walking and I'm running, and yet I still can't reach her. I don't understand why I can't reach her. Why won't she just turn around?

"Mom, please!" I scream at the top of my lungs.

Digging my feet into the sand, I push myself as hard as I can. My feet smack roughly onto the wet sand, and I can feel rocks and shells digging into my skin but it doesn't matter. The only thing that hurts right now is that she won't acknowledge me. She doesn't understand that I'm right behind her. If she would just turn around and see me, I know she would stop. She would stop and she would smile and she would take me into her arms and never let go.

The tears fall steadily down my cheeks as I watch her get to the rocks and begin climbing over them.

"Mom, stop! Please, don't go! Don't leave me!" I cry.

I'm still running but I'm not going anywhere. I'm not getting any closer. She's too far away now, and I know I'll never make it to her.

She's already at the top of the rocks and making her way down the other side. I watch in horror as her blonde head disappears from sight.

She's gone. She was right here in front of me, and I let her get away.

Glancing down at my feet, I realize I'm not running anymore. Looking behind me to see how far I've come, I don't see any of my footprints in the sand, and I wonder if I ever even left this spot. Did I just stand here doing nothing? It felt like I was running, like I was moving forward, but maybe I never was. Maybe this entire time I was just standing still while everything around me continued to move forward. Looking back at the rocks where she disappeared, I realize I that I don't want to be left behind.

Jerking up in bed on a gasp, I quickly glance around me, trying to get my bearings. When I see the familiar surroundings of my bedroom, I place my hand over my heart and slow my breathing.

The dream felt so real. I can still feel the wet sand on my feet and the smell of the ocean in the air. Reaching my hand up to my cheek, it's wet from the tears I cried while I slept. It's the same reoccurring dream I've had since she died. The dream left me for a little while, but tonight it came back with a vengeance. I lost count how many times I've watched her walk away from me in my dreams while I scream for her. I continue to scream and push myself and hurt myself and the results never change; she doesn't turn around, and she doesn't let me come with her. The definition of insanity is doing the same thing over and over again and expecting different results. She's gone and she's never coming back. I can't reach her, I can't touch her again, and I can't stop her from leaving. Hurting myself and everyone around me because I can't move on is insane. Expecting my life to get better on its own when I want nothing more than to be with her again is insane.

I reach over to my bedside table and flip on the lamp, my eyes immediately zeroing in on the napkins littering my bed. When I came home from the cemetery, I walked to my door and paused in shock when I saw that it was entirely covered with napkins. Taped from top to bottom, covering every inch, were notes from Zander. I read each and every one of them before carefully taking them all down and bringing them inside with me.

I fell asleep surrounded by them after having read them each a hundred times. Picking up the one closest to me, I stare at the words he wrote in black pen.

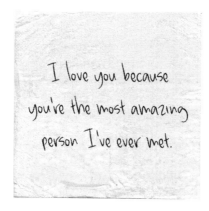

Setting it down and picking up another one, I scan the words and think about him sitting at his kitchen table with his head bent over the napkins while he writes the words that are in his heart. I read through each and every one again and again and let his words fill my heart.

I love you because you make me smile.
I love you because you trusted me to keep you safe.
I love you because you make delicious cupcakes.
I love you because you're stronger than you know.
I love you because you're beautiful.
I love you because you make me happier than I've ever been.
I love you because you're not afraid to dream.
I love you because someday, you will write your story...and it will be amazing.

When I get to the last one, I look up and stare at the old ones from him I still have tacked to the bulletin board, scanning each and every one of those as well until I get to one tacked right in the middle. Goosebumps form on my arms and a chill runs down my spine when I see a note that wasn't there when I came home from the cemetery and fell asleep on top of my covers, fully clothed, surrounded by Zander's words.

Swinging my legs over the side of the bed, I get up slowly and make my way across the room until I'm standing right in front of the board. My vision blurs from the tears, and I clamp my hand over my mouth to keep the sobs in when I realize I'm not seeing things.

How is this possible? I crumpled this up and threw it into the grass at the cemetery.

With a shaking hand, I reach out and touch the note to see if it's real. When I feel the rough texture of the napkin under my fingertips, the hand against my mouth can no longer contain my sobs.

I let everything out that I've been holding in for so long. I cry until I'm taking hiccupping breaths and my head aches and my eyes feel puffy. I stare at the note, the handwriting, and the message, and for the first time in a long time, I laugh through my tears. I laugh because I'm all cried out. I laugh because my heart feels like it's going to burst. I laugh because I'm probably going crazy but it doesn't matter. Nothing matters but the note, what it says, and the impossibility of it being in my room right now when I threw it away.

Turning away from the board, I race over to my computer, sit down and power it up.

As I wait for my word processing software to load, I wipe away my tears and think about the words Zander said to me that day in the park with Luke.

"It's the bumps and the bruises, the pain and the fear; it's messy and it's real and it's not some perfect little story that can be tied up in a bow. It's exactly what you should write about."

I hear his voice encouraging me to do something I've thought about but never had the strength to do. I see his smiling face in my mind, and it gives me the boost I need to do this.

Placing my hands over the keys on my laptop, I type the first sentence—words that I've repeated over and over in my head. My fingers fly over the keys and the story pours out of me along with more tears. I make it real and I make it raw, and I expose every single part of myself that I've kept locked up tight.

For two days I sit at my computer. For two days I relive every part of the last year and a half, and for once it doesn't break me. I forget to eat, I barely sleep; I do nothing but type. I type until my fingers are sore and my head aches from crying and staring at the small computer screen. I type until the very last word leaves me. When I finish, I look back through what I've done and realize I've written a book. Not a short story, or a play…a book. An entire book about my life.

I know I should eat something, or at the very least take a nap, but I can't. There's someplace very important I need to be, and a nap will have to wait. Hitting the "print" button on my computer, I jump in the shower while the pages spit out, one after another.

When I'm done with my shower and the printer has released the final page, I secure the stack with a rubber band. Running into my room to grab my purse, I glance quickly at my bulletin board. Taking a deep breath, I remove the one napkin from the center of the board and slide it under the rubber band, running my palm over it and smiling, then quickly turn to my bed and grab the most important one from Zander.

Jumping into my car, I race across town, glancing over at the pages stacked on my passenger seat every few seconds. I pull into the driveway, and when I don't see his car, I try not to let it upset me. Grabbing a pen and the napkin from Zander I brought with me, I quickly scribble a note underneath his words and stick it under the rubber band next to the other napkin from my bulletin board. Scooping the stack of pages up into my arms, I get out of the car. With a deep breath, I walk to the top of the stairs of the front porch. I squat down and place the rubber band wrapped pages right on top of his welcome mat.

Standing back up, I look down one last time at the napkin with both of our messages on it.

I love you because someday,
you will write your story...
and it will be amazing.

Zander:

I'm sorry. Thank you for believing in me.

I love you.

Addison

Chapter Twenty
Brave

Three months later.

Sitting at my desk by the window, I finish typing the last sentence of my paragraph and hit *save*. Closing my eyes and stretching my arms above my head, I work out the kinks in my shoulder from sitting so long. When I open my eyes again a few minutes later, I glance down at my computer and smile. On top of my keyboard is a napkin, and I laugh when I read the words.

> Smile. I love you.
> Come into the kitchen.
> I have a surprise.

I've lost count of how many napkins I have now. I still keep each and every one of them, but they're no longer tacked to my bulletin board since I ran out of room on that thing a long time ago. Looking over at the wall where the board used to hang, I sigh and smile again when I see the only note that hangs there now. It's in a glass frame that Zander bought for me as soon as he finished reading my story a few months ago. Getting up from my computer chair, I walk over to the frame and stare at it, thinking about the day I found that napkin taped to the wall of Dr. Thompson's empty office, and then the day I found it again. The words don't fill me with confusion or sadness anymore. When I read them, I think about the impossible and how if you're lucky enough and loved enough, sometimes incomprehensible, amazing things can happen to you.

Running my fingertips over the smooth glass, I silently read the words to myself.

I take a deep breath as I smile at the words and the drawing of the stick figure with arms open wide, dropping my hand from the glass, and back away from the wall. Glancing over at my computer, I know it's time to do something I've been putting off for far too long. I quickly walk back over to my desk and lean down, opening up a browser window and logging into Facebook. I go to her page and the sight of her profile picture no longer fills me with pain. Clicking on the *Account Settings* menu, I go right to the *Security* section.

"I love you," I whisper as I click *Deactivate Account.*

Stepping away from the computer, I take a deep breath before turning away and heading out into the kitchen.

"It's about time you got here. I slaved over dinner and it was going to start getting cold," Zander tells me as he meets me by the doorway and pulls me into his arms. I look over at the table and see that it's littered with Chinese takeout containers.

"Slaved, huh?" I ask with a laugh.

He bends down and presses his lips to mine. Reaching up, I wrap my arms around the back of his neck and pull him closer. The kiss ends all too soon, and he rests his forehead against mine and looks into my eyes.

"You have no idea how hard it is to order Chinese. There's so many choices to pick from," he jokes.

We pull apart and make our way over to the table to start dishing out food. While we eat and talk about his day at work and my day writing, I think about how we got here and how truly happy I am for the first time in my life.

After I left my story on Zander's front porch three months ago, I immediately drove to my parents' house. Even though I had told my father I was done, I needed to make sure he understood what all that entailed. When I walked back into the house, I found him packing a suitcase. He was going back to rehab and he told me he was finished making me promises he couldn't keep. I told him I was finished with the bakery. I couldn't run it anymore while he was gone; I didn't *want* to run it anymore. It wasn't my dream, and I couldn't go one more day doing something that didn't make me happy.

Within a few weeks, Snow's Sugary Sweets was sold to a nice young couple that promised to keep it exactly like my mother had it and would continue to use all of her recipes. They even agreed to keep Meg on staff while she went back to school to finish her degree in Elementary Education.

I talk to my father once a week, and I don't allow myself to get wrapped up in his problem anymore. I try my best to let him know that I support him, but I don't let his choices affect my life like they used to. I don't know what will happen between us when he gets out of rehab this time, but with Zander's help, I don't let myself worry about something I have no control over.

Staring at Zander across the table, I can't help but smile as he talks animatedly about a patient he had to X-ray that day. When I left those pages on his doorstep, I wasn't sure if I would ever hear from him again. I had no idea if I'd pushed him too far away or whether or not he'd finally realized I wasn't worth the trouble.

For the rest of that day, I forced myself not to dwell on it. I wouldn't allow myself to be nervous that he was at home reading my words and finally knowing everything about me. After speaking with my father, I went to the bakery and spent the night making every single one of my mother's recipes. I baked muffins and pies, cakes and cookies, and a hundred other things that I grew up eating and making side-by-side with her. At eleven o'clock, long after the shop had closed, the back door opened, and I held my breath when I saw Zander walk in carrying my story under his arm.

"Holy shit," he whispered, looking around at all of the baked goods that covered every surface of the kitchen.

I laughed nervously as he stood just inside the doorway.

"I got a little carried away," I told him with a shrug.

His eyes locked onto mine, and I watched as he walked toward me. Butterflies filled my stomach as he stepped around the island in the middle of the room and came right up to me. He set the pile of papers on the counter next to me and then finally reached up and put both of his hands on either side of my face. I leaned my body closer to his and looked up at his face.

"Thank you for trusting me with your story."

I didn't hesitate to wrap my arms around his waist.

"Thank you reading it. And for forgiving me," I whispered.

He shook his head at me and rubbed his thumbs against my cheek.

"There's nothing to forgive. You deserved more from me. You deserved the truth, and I was too afraid to give it to you," he replied.

I glanced away from him and down at my story on the counter.

"I was afraid too. I didn't want you to know all of this and look at me differently," I admitted.

"Don't you understand?" he asked as he removed on left hand from around his neck and kissed my scar. "That story right there, it's your heart and soul, and it's the reason why I love you. Every single word is why I fell in love with you, and it's why I could never, ever stop loving you no matter what. You amaze me, Addison. Your strength amazes me, and the fact that you love me back amazes me. At least I hope you still love me back," he said nervously as he bit his bottom lip.

"And I thought I was the crazy one," I told him with a laugh. "How could I not love you? You were her friend. She trusted you with me, and you did everything you could to teach me how to live again. I love you. I don't want to be stuck in the past anymore. I want to finally look forward to the future, and I want to do it with you. I need you to keep me strong."

He placed a soft kiss on the tip of my nose and then smiled down at me.

"You don't need me for anything, Sugar. That story right there proves just how strong you really are. You can do anything you set your mind to, and there's nowhere else I'd rather be than by your side watching your dreams come true."

The last three months have been the best and the scariest of my life. Upon Zander's insistence, I submitted my story to a literary agent. In the meantime, with the money from the sale of the bakery, I enrolled in the local community college and began taking English and creative writing classes while I continued to write more stories.

"Oh my gosh, I almost forgot your surprise," Zander says as he wipes his hands on a napkin and gets up from the table. I watch as he walks over to the counter and picks up a large manila envelope and hands it over to me.

"Don't be mad but I already opened it. I kind of knew what it was, but I wanted to make sure before you saw it," he tells me as I take the package from his hands and flip it over.

"What is this?" I ask as I lift up the already torn flap on the envelope.

"Remember how I told you that one of my patients last month works for a publisher in New York?" he asks as my hand reaches inside the package.

"Yes. And if I remember correctly, I told you not to bother him," I tell Zander as I raise my eyebrow at him and silently scold him with my look.

"I think you should know by now that I never do anything you tell me to," he says with a laugh.

Shaking my head at him, I grab the thick packet of papers inside the envelope and slide them out. I gasp when I see the title page to my story.

"Oh my God," I mumble as I run my hand over the top page that looks like it's been professionally formatted and bound together.

"They're going to publish it, Sugar. They loved every single word," Zander tells me excitedly.

I stare down at the manuscript in my hands, and I can hardly believe this is happening. I almost lost myself, and this story was so close to never being written. And now other people will read it. It will sit on the shelves of bookstores and someone will pick it up and read about a girl who almost gave up on everything. With the help of a boy who loved her more than she thought possible, and the eyes of the most important person in her life watching over her, she learned how to move forward.

She learned how to live.

Epilogue

Ten years later…

"Mommy, was Grandma at your wedding when you married Daddy?"

I smile down at Angel, my six-year-old daughter, curled up next to my side on the couch as she flips through our wedding album.

"No, Sweets, she wasn't there in person. But I'm sure she was looking down on us from Heaven."

Angel looks up at me with her big, gorgeous, gray eyes—mine and my mother's eyes all rolled into one.

"She's an angel in Heaven and that's why you named me Angel, right?" she asks with the innocence of a child.

"That's right! And even though she's not here, she loves us and she's watching over all of us and keeping us safe."

She goes back to the photo album and intently stares at each and every picture. I hug her closer to my side and kiss the top of her head.

It seems like so long ago that I swore I would never have children because I couldn't bear the thought of doing it without my mother here to guide me and shower them with love. But now, I don't know how I ever thought a life without children would be worth living. Glancing up at the framed napkin that still hangs on the wall and has followed me and Zander to each of the places we've lived, I close my eyes and send a silent "thank you" up to Heaven.

When I first found that note, I couldn't possibly comprehend how it was possible for something like that to happen. I tried not to dwell on the fact that I had no idea where the note came from or how it was conceivable for me to be holding something like that in my hand. It wasn't until Angel was born and I became a mother myself that I finally let all of the doubts go and just accepted the fact that somehow, someway, my mother was watching over me. I still don't know if Dr. Thompson was real or if she was sent by my mother to help me, but I don't question it anymore. I get it now. The moment the doctor put Angel in my arms, I instantly fell in love with her and the bond between us was forged, never to be broken—even in death. I knew that no matter what, I would always protect her, and even if I couldn't be with her, I would never be far away.

I still miss my mother every day. I still think about her more often than not, and I still wish she was here with me helping me through life. I still wonder why she had to go and have finally come to terms with the fact that it was just her time. It doesn't hurt as much to think about her anymore. Remembering her face and her voice and her hugs don't leave me feeling empty and lonely. They leave me feeling lucky and loved to have had her in my life, even though the time we had together wasn't nearly long enough. I'm the person I am today because she loved me. I will continue being strong and live my life to the fullest because that's what she taught me to do. And now that I have a daughter, I have an even bigger reason to enjoy everything that life brings me.

"Sugar, I'm home!" Zander shouts from kitchen as he makes his way to us in the living room.

He walks up behind the couch, and I tip my head back so I can see him. Leaning over me, he places a kiss on my lips and then moves over to our daughter, scooping her up and over the back of the couch while she squeals in delight.

"Hey there, Baby Sugar, how was your day?" he asks her as he peppers her face with kisses.

"Mommy and I were talking about Grandma and how she's watching over me. Do you think she watches me when I go to the bathroom? I hope not. There are just some things that people don't need to see."

Zander and I burst out laughing at our daughter's choice of words, and I can't help but think back to the conversation I had with my mom about the very same thing.

"I'm sure Grandma gives you your privacy when you go to the bathroom," Zander says with another laugh as he sets Angel down and then pulls a large, thick envelope out from behind his back.

"Oooooh, is that a present for me?" Angel asks excitedly.

"Sorry, Baby Sugar, this one is for mommy," he replies, coming around to the front of the couch and placing it on my lap before sitting down next to me.

I notice the return address from my publisher and wonder if it's a copy of my newest manuscript. Tearing into the envelope, I pull out a note on their letterhead and scan through the words.

"Oh my gosh, it's the ten year anniversary of my first book. They had a special hardcover edition printed for me," I whisper softly to Zander as I reach my hand inside and pull out the book.

Staring at the cover, I run my hand gently over the title and remember the days I spent locked away in my apartment, finally letting everything out and putting it down on paper.

"Congratulations, Sugar. You've come a long way and I'm so proud of you," Zander tells me, placing a kiss on top of my head.

I've written more books than I can count over the years and each one has brought me success that I never imagined. But this one, the story of my life, will always have a special place in my heart.

Opening the hard cover, I flip past the title page, and I smile down at the first few words of the prologue that I typed so long ago.

Death changes everyone...

The End
✝

If you or someone you know has persistent feelings of sadness, hopelessness, and thoughts of suicide, it's important to reach out for help. Asking for help is not a sign of weakness. If you are feeling overwhelmed, or if suicide seems like an option, you can always talk to someone you love or a health professional.

Suicide is never the only option.

If you or someone you know is contemplating suicide, please call 911 or contact the National Suicide Prevention Lifeline at 1-800-273-TALK or http://www.suicidepreventionlifeline.org/GetHelp

Acknowledgements

First and foremost, thank you to Buffy and Madison. You were the first ones to read the couple of chapters I was playing around with a year ago. You were the first ones to get a glimpse into this story, and you convinced me that I had to write it. I wasn't sure if I ever wanted anyone to read this. I'm still not sure! But with your love and support, this story came to light. I am so thankful to have both of you in my life. Thank you for encouraging me and believing in me.

Max. Oh, Max. Where would I be without you? I'd be stuck in the hell of past/present tense, and I would have never known the beauty of Supernatural! I love you. Thank you for writing a bio that spoke to my soul two years ago so I could find you! Thank you for helping me with this story and for helping me grow as a writer. FYI, Ackles is mine.

Tiffany King and Jasinda Wilder— Thank you so much for your early read of this story and for your constant support and friendship.

James, Madelyn, and Drew—Thank you for letting me be emo for months about this story. Thank you for giving me hugs and kisses when you saw I needed them. Thank you for loving me unconditionally even though I forget to feed you and call you by the wrong names.

Andrea—Thank you for being the best mother-in-law in the world. Thank you for your faith in me and your continued support. Thank you for being proud of me and for being my family. I love you and I am so thankful to have you in my life.

Last, but certainly not least - Thank you to the fans for taking a chance on me. Thank you for loving my funny and following me with the serious. Thank you for being the best fans in the world!

Cover by Okay Creations—www.okaycreations.com

Editing by Polished Pen—www.polished-pen.com

Formatting by Fictional Formats—

https://www.facebook.com/pages/Fictional-formats

Made in the USA
San Bernardino, CA
24 June 2013